A LIFE LIKE THE REST

Kevin Arkadie

BROADWAY PLAY PUBLISHING INC
New York
www.broadwayplaypublishing.com
info@broadwayplaypublishing.com

First edition: August 2024
I S B N: 979-8-88856-029-7

Book design: Marie Donovan
Page make-up: Adobe InDesign
Typeface: Palatino

A LIFE LIKE THE REST premiered on 30 January
1986, produced by Frederick Douglass Creative Arts
Center Inc, (Fred Hudson, Producer) at the Judith
Anderson Theater in New York. The cast and creative
contributors were:

JONATHAN .... Jonathan Earl Peck
KYLE .... Brian Thomas
MAUREEN .... Melissa Fonts
PHIL .... Willie C Carpenter
MARGIE .... Barbara Clarke
VICKY .... Victoria Gabriel Platt

Director .... Dean Kirby
Set design .... Charles McClennahan
Costume design .... Anita Ellis
Lighting design .... Victor En Yu Tan
Sound design .... Bill Dreisbach
Production Stage Manager .... Jesse Wooden Jr

CHARACTERS & SETTING

JONATHAN, 20s. Cynically idealistic. Energy to burn, or maybe it's just angst and worry. Nothing he can't do if he sets his mind to it, at least that's what he tells himself.

VICKEY, 13. Precocious. Open and full of enthusiasm. Intellectually very bright, but like her older brother, she disguises it as "country sense".

KYLE, 15. Stocky, muscular. Down Syndrome. His emotions are impulsive and unrestrained. He loves deeply and wholeheartedly.

MARJORIE, 40s. Full of worry and contemplation. Frays at the edges, gets overwhelmed from time to time, but there's an earthy practicalness to her that belies her cognitive disablility.

PHIL, 40s. Tall and lanky, proud that he's the patriarch of the family, but aware of his limitations. Cognitive disability, but capable of being stoic and warm at the same time.

MAUREEN, 20s. Officious, yet earnest and compassionate. Not as stoic as she pretends.

Time and Place: 1970s, rural Virginia

Setting: A small, secluded two story wood framed cabin

ACT ONE

Scene 1

(Afternoon. It is the main room of the cabin. It should be spacious with enough room for a sofa, a television set, a desk for JONATHAN, *and an easy chair or two. The dining room is a continuation of the living room and there should be a dining table and a credenza. A swinging door leads off to the kitchen. He talks on the telephone, playing with a "Newton's Cradle" —five steel balls on a pendulum, "click-clacking" to demonstrate Newton's theory that to every action there is an opposite reaction.)*

JONATHAN: I want to get a license—for the Renaissance Fair—how much is it? How do you expect anyone to turn a profit charging fees like these? Send me all the stuff anyway, I mean, one way or the other we're gonna be there. No, there's nothing you can do to change my mind. Thanks. Bye.

*(*JONATHAN *hangs up, waits for the "click-clacking" of the Newton's Cradle to stop, filters through items on his desk. Visible is a large "Renaissance Fair" poster which hangs on a wall.* VICKEY *enters through front door carrying school books.)*

VICKEY: A water pipe broke at school. None of the toilets were working so they let us all go home early.

JONATHAN: Really?

VICKEY: Cross my heart and hope to— (*Seeing the TV*) Oh, we got a new TV! I ain't even gonna have to miss a single episode of All My Children. That was fast, it didn't even take a week this time. Can I turn it on, Johnny, huh, can I? (*Crossing to TV*) Hey, this one's broken already, the turn-on switch is missing. What's that you're holding, Johnny? Johnny, I can't turn the TV on—help me.

JONATHAN: It works by remote control.

VICKEY: Oh. Turn it on.

JONATHAN: Don't you have some studying to do?

VICKEY: I don't feel like studying, I feel like watching TV.

JONATHAN: And if you feel like throwing a vase through the picture tube are you going to do that?

VICKEY: I don't feel like doin' that now.

JONATHAN: Vickey, things are getting real tough—this is the last TV we're gonna be able to get for a while, and the same goes for everything else. We have to be careful with things. Do you understand?

VICKEY: You mean I can't watch TV when I want to? That's not fair!

JONATHAN: It's fair enough until you learn not to break things.

VICKEY: Fuck you, Johnny.

JONATHAN: I dare you to say that again.

(*Beat*)

VICKEY: It's one o'clock, Johnny. Cartoons are on at one o'clock but I never get to watch em. Can I watch cartoons?

JONATHAN: No, not until—

VICKEY: I want to watch TV, Johnny! I won't do that again, I promise! I'm sorry, Johnny, I'm sorry! Can I watch, huh, please?

JONATHAN: Vickey—

VICKEY: I want to watch TV!! (*Realizing this is getting her nowhere*) I didn't mean it.

JONATHAN: You saw somebody do that, didn't you? Who was it? Tell me.

VICKEY: Billy Tucker. We were at that junk-yard behind Murphy's field. We were playin' and we found this old TV set and Billy says, "Watch this," and he threw a rock right through that TV.

JONATHAN: I don't understand you, Vickey.

VICKEY: What's to understand? Mister Rogers was on TV and I hate him, he's sick. Margie and Phil were hugging and everything and Kyle was laughing, I just wanted them to be quiet.

JONATHAN: Next time you just ask them, all right? All right?

VICKEY: All right.

JONATHAN: If you don't like Mister Rogers, for God's sake, don't watch him—and I don't want you playing around in that junk yard anymore.

VICKEY: Okay. (*She sulks.*)

JONATHAN: (*Feeling sorry*) How you feeling? Okay?

VICKEY: Yeah—Johnny?

JONATHAN: Yes?

VICKEY: Since I can't watch TV, can I have a pair of rollerskates?

JONATHAN: Rollerskates?

VICKEY: Yeah, I saw this magazine ad and Linda Ronstadt and Olivia Newton-John were on roller skates. Since I'm gonna be a star when I grow up I think I should get a pair, don't you?

JONATHAN: I don't know, Vickey, look what you did to the TV.

VICKEY: Please?

JONATHAN: I'll see what I can do, but if I get 'em you'll have to take care of them.

VICKEY: I will, I promise.

(VICKEY *hugs* JONATHAN.)

VICKEY: I love you, Johnny!

JONATHAN: I love you, too, Vickey. Now, you still got some studyin' to do, don't you?

VICKEY: Do I have to?

JONATHAN: Yeah. You wanna cook dinner tonight?

VICKEY: Rollerskates?

JONATHAN: I'll try.

VICKEY: Sure, I'll cook.

(JONATHAN *playfully embraces* VICKEY *in a headlock.*)

JONATHAN: That's my girl. Now, get to your homework.

(VICKEY *begins up the stairs.*)

JONATHAN: Will you tell Phil and Margie to come down for a second. Tell them it's real important.

VICKEY: Okay, Johnny.

(VICKEY *exits.* JONATHAN *crosses to desk.*)

JONATHAN: Kyle?

(PHIL *enters from upstairs.*)

JONATHAN: Phil. Where's Margie?

PHIL: Yes, she's coming. Lots of pots today, John, they's real pretty.

JONATHAN: That's wonderful, Phil. How many did you make today?

PHIL: How many?

JONATHAN: Yes, Phil, tell me how many pots you made today.

PHIL: Three or four.

JONATHAN: Very good!

PHIL: Margie helped me.

JONATHAN: You and Margie are a good team, Phil.

PHIL: Do you really think so, John? We's a good team, huh?

JONATHAN: The best I ever saw.

PHIL: Ya like us, don't ya, John?

JONATHAN: Very much, Phil. Phil, why didn't you bring one of the pots down so I could see it?

PHIL: I don't know.

JONATHAN: Is Margie gonna bring one when she comes down?

PHIL: Yes, Margie's coming.

JONATHAN: Will you get Margie for me, Phil?

PHIL: *(Yelling)* Margie! Margie!

JONATHAN: Great, Phil.

(PHIL *snickers.)*

JONATHAN: Kyle told me you had a phone call yesterday while I was gone. Do you remember anything about that?

PHIL: A phone call?

JONATHAN: Uh-huh.

PHIL: On the telephone, huh?

JONATHAN: Yes, Kyle says that you and Margie talked to someone.

(MARGIE *enters from upstairs.*)

MARGIE: Ya ain't mad at us, is ya, Johnny?

JONATHAN: Now don't be thinkin' that I'm mad, I'm not, but I want to know if you and Phil had a phone call yesterday.

MARGIE: A phone call? Yes, the phone did ring yesterday while I was working. It rang and rang and rang and rang!

PHIL: Yeah!

(MARGIE *and* PHIL *imitate the sound of the phone.*)

JONATHAN: Which one of you answered the phone? Margie? Phil?

(MARGIE *and* PHIL *stop ringing.*)

MARGIE: Margie, Margie, Margie.

JONATHAN: Margie, did you?

MARGIE: Yeah.

JONATHAN: Who was it?

MARGIE: I don't know—a lady.

JONATHAN: What was the lady's name?

MARGIE: I don't know.

JONATHAN: Did you take a message like I showed you?

MARGIE: Phil.

JONATHAN: Phil, did you take a message?

PHIL: No, Margie did.

MARGIE: I took it, and she talked to me and I wrote it all down.

JONATHAN: Good. Now tell me where the message is.

MARGIE: I don't know.

PHIL laughs.

JONATHAN: Be quiet, Phil. *(To* MARGIE*)* Try to remember, Margie.

MARGIE: I don't remember! I can't, I can't, I can't!

JONATHAN: It's all right, don't worry about it. Why don't you and Phil go on upstairs now and see if your pots are drying. Phil, I want to see one when they're dry, okay?

PHIL: Is ya mad at us, John?

JONATHAN: No, I ain't mad.

PHIL: It were Margie, it weren't me.

JONATHAN: I'm not mad at either of ya.

PHIL: Are ya sure?

JONATHAN: I'm not mad.

MARGIE: I can't remember, Johnny, I really can't.

JONATHAN: It's all right, I'm not angry, now go.

*(*MARGIE *and* PHIL *exit.)*

JONATHAN: I'm just a little disappointed.

*(*JONATHAN *looks around the room for the message. Quits.* KYLE *enters from kitchen dribbling a basketball. He wears shorts and a T-shirt.)*

KYLE: Play with me.

JONATHAN: Kyle, we have work to do. I gotta chop some wood.

*(*KYLE *is absorbed in dribbling the basketball.)*

JONATHAN: You coming?

*(*JONATHAN *exits through the kitchen.* KYLE *dribbles after him.* VICKEY *enters from upstairs, vamps her way towards*

TV, rubs her hands across the tube. She exits through front door. After several moments someone knocks at the door. The knock repeats. MAUREEN *enters.)*

MAUREEN: Hello! Anybody home?

(MAUREEN *looks about the living room nosily, then looks through kitchen door.)*

MAUREEN: Hello? Young boy? Would you come here? Here. I want to talk with you.

(KYLE *enters. Seeing* MAUREEN *he loses all focus on the basketball and puts it on her.)*

MAUREEN: Hello there.

KYLE: Hi.

(MAUREEN *dribbles the basketball.* KYLE *claps.)*

MAUREEN: That's a nice basketball you have there, is it new?

KYLE: Yes.

MAUREEN: It's neat. What's your name?

(KYLE *laughs.)*

MAUREEN: Don't you want to tell me your name? Is it a secret? C'mon, you can trust me, I won't tell.

KYLE: Kyle.

MAUREEN: Kyle?

KYLE: Yeah.

MAUREEN: Well, I'm very glad to meet you, Kyle. My name is Maureen.

KYLE: Reen?

MAUREEN: Maureen. Can you say Maureen?

KYLE: Reen!

MAUREEN: That's very good! Is anyone else home besides you? Are your mommy and daddy home?

KYLE: It's a very nice basketball.

KYLE: Watch. *(He dribbles the ball for her.)*

MAUREEN: Bravo, you're real good at that!

KYLE: Yes!

MAUREEN: Kyle? Kyle?

KYLE: Yes, Reen?

MAUREEN: Where's your mommy and daddy?

KYLE: You want John?

MAUREEN: Is John your daddy? Is that your daddy?

KYLE: Do you like me, Reen?

MAUREEN: Yes, I do.

KYLE: Do you really like me?

MAUREEN: Yes, I really do.

KYLE: Will you hug me?

MAUREEN: Sure, I will.

(MAUREEN hugs KYLE but he refuses to let go.)

MAUREEN: Kyle? Let go, Kyle.

(JONATHAN enters, dirty from chopping wood. He affects his behavior to seem retarded.)

JONATHAN: Tap him on the back.

(MAUREEN does. KYLE lets go.)

MAUREEN: Thank you. Who are you?

JONATHAN: John.

MAUREEN: You're John? Maybe you can help me—are your mommy and daddy home? Are your parents here?

JONATHAN: Polly want a cracker?

MAUREEN: Not parrots, John, parents—mommy and daddy.

KYLE: *(Laughing)* John funny! John funny!

MAUREEN: How about Dr Fleming? Is he here?

(JONATHAN *and* KYLE *come to attention.*)

MAUREEN: I'm looking for Dr Fleming, John, do you know where he is?

JONATHAN: He's not here.

MAUREEN: Well, someone must be here. John, I want to look around, can I look around? Will you show me?

JONATHAN: I can't!

MARGIE: Why not, John?

JONATHAN doesn't answer.

MAUREEN: Kyle, will you show me about the house? I want to find Mommy and Daddy?

(KYLE *points through a window.*)

KYLE: Look, Reen, look!

MAUREEN: A basketball court, that's nice.

KYLE: Come.

(KYLE *tugs* MAUREEN *by the arm through the kitchen.* JONATHAN *immediately rummages through her purse and attaché which she has left.* MAUREEN *re-enters.*)

MAUREEN: It's a good thing I came back. You shouldn't go through people's belongings.

JONATHAN: *(Mock sulking)* I'm sorry.

MAUREEN: It's all right, I'm not angry with you.

(MAUREEN *hugs* JONATHAN.)

MAUREEN: Feel better?

JONATHAN: Yeah.

(MAUREEN *crosses to stairwell.*)

MAUREEN: Hello! I can't believe they'd leave you here by yourselves.

(JONATHAN *nods yes.* KYLE *enters.*)

MAUREEN: Kyle, you showed me your basketball court, now show me upstairs, okay?

(KYLE *shakes his head "no".*)

MAUREEN: Why not, Kyle?

(KYLE *points to* JONATHAN.)

JONATHAN: I can tell you exactly what's up there. Four rooms, one bathroom and an attic. The attic is converted into a workroom. There you'll find Phil and Margie, and in one of the other rooms my little sister is doing her homework.

MAUREEN: Kyle, excuse me and John for a minute. Go shoot some baskets or something—practice your jump shot like I showed you—one hand?

JONATHAN: Kyle, go and finish stacking the wood.

KYLE: 'Kay. (*He exits.*)

MAUREEN: John, I'm going to tell you a little story. Do you know the time? It is after one. I arrived in town this morning before eight and I have spent all day trying to find this house, continually being herked and jerked around by everyone I came across. Locals say they've never heard of this house or they say it's over in the next county, and the ones who said they knew gave me the wrong directions, I'm beginning to believe intentionally. Five hours I drive around these woods—I run out of gas, I walk back to town because no one will give me a ride, and I'm totally exhausted. I arrive here at my intended destination and you act like a— (*Catching herself*) Who the hell do you think you are?!

JONATHAN: I'm John. Who are you?

MAUREEN: Maureen. Why did you pretend that you were—

JONATHAN: *Retarded?* Because I don't trust people who walk into my house unannounced. What do you want, Maureen?

MAUREEN: I've been assigned to you. I'm from the State. Your social worker.

JONATHAN: We don't have a social worker.

MAUREEN: You do now.

JONATHAN: We don't need a social worker.

MAUREEN: Everyone needs a social worker. Your file was lost, they found it, they gave it to me—rummaging through my purse you should have discovered that.

JONATHAN: I didn't have enough time.

MAUREEN: Asking a question would have been more expedient.

JONATHAN: But not as much fun. *(A thought)* How did you find us? Nobody in town would tell you.

MAUREEN: Mr Sayer told me.

JONATHAN: Jeb Sayer? He must have been out of buckshot to let you get close enough to actually talk to him.

MAUREEN: You know him?

JONATHAN: I know that since his wife died last year he just lays around the house all day. Losing his leg didn't help, either.

MAUREEN: He needs an artificial one. He won't get fitted and promises to burn the generic one I brought him. Burning things is not the solution to sadness.

JONATHAN: You have a solution?

MAUREEN: Work. Caring for others. Improving other lives is the best way to improve your own.

JONATHAN: How social of you.

MAUREEN: There's no sense a human being living the way he is. There's nothing wrong with a prosthetic leg.

JONATHAN: I'll keep that in mind.

MAUREEN: He gave me your address to get rid of me.

JONATHAN: I've got some addresses for you.

(Beat)

MAUREEN: I left something in my car.

JONATHAN: These?

(JONATHAN tosses MAUREEN the pack of Marlboro Lights he lifted from her purse. She's a mix of contrasting emotions.)

JONATHAN: Why don't we just complete your business and then you can smoke all the way back to Richmond.

(VICKEY enters through front door with a walking cane that's been burned down to little more than a nub.)

VICKEY: I found this burned up cane on the porch, and I saw Jeb Sayer hopping up the trail behind the house. *(Noticing MAUREEN)* Whoa! *Civilization.* Hello. I'm Victoria, but call me Vickey, I hate Victoria. As a matter of fact I shouldn't have told you it was my name, I should have said it was Eunice or something.

MAUREEN: I'm Maureen.

VICKEY: *(Re the cane)* Why'd you burn this?

MAUREEN: It was for Mr Sayers' until I get him fitted for a new leg.

JONATHAN: He doesn't seem to want a new leg.

MAUREEN: I'm not giving up.

(VICKEY looks through the living room window.)

VICKEY: He's faster than me getting back to his house, he don't need another leg.

(MAUREEN *steps out onto the porch.*)

MAUREEN: (*Off*) I see you, Mr Sayer. I figured you'd do something like this. That's why I brought two!

(MAUREEN *re-enters.*)

JONATHAN: If he doesn't want your leg, why are you trying to force him to take it?

MAUREEN: His life will be better.

JONATHAN: You're certain?

MAUREEN: Positive.

VICKEY: Can I watch TV now, Johnny?

JONATHAN: When are you going to start supper? Margie and Phil are probably starving.

VICKEY: I'd be starving, too, if I were up there screwin' all day.

JONATHAN: (*To* MAUREEN) Uh—she means screwin' around—what they're doing—actually—is making pottery for the County Renaissance Fair that comes every year. It's their first year so they're working particularly hard. They're getting a lot of good work done. They hardly ever stop.

VICKEY: Screwin'.

JONATHAN: *Around.*

VICKEY: (*To* MAUREEN) Will you be my friend? Will you do things with me? Are you a social worker?

MAUREEN: Yes.

VICKEY: Never mind. I bet you want information from us, don't ya?

MAUREEN: (*To* JONATHAN) How about a way to reach Dr Fleming? I've been trying to make an appointment with him for weeks. I asked several locals and they directed me to 13121 Old River Road—there's nothing there but a—

JONATHAN: Cemetery.

MAUREEN: I see.

JONATHAN: George Fleming's not very talkative these days, you have to dig things out of him. That's not to say he never was talkative, he used to go on and on espousing theories and hypotheses and justifications— he's just a tad quieter these days.

(*Confused silence*)

MAUREEN: When did he pass away?

VICKEY: He hasn't passed away, he's dead! That's what Johnny says. Two years ago.

MAUREEN: You're wards of the State assigned to his care. I have recent documentation in my files signed by—*you.*

JONATHAN: Vickey, maybe Miss uhh—

MAUREEN: Jankowski.

JONATHAN: What?

MAUREEN: Jankowski. Maureen Jankowski. It's Polish.

JONATHAN: Miss Jankowski is dying to smoke a cigarette. Let's offer her some tea, instead.

MAUREEN: Tea would be nice.

JONATHAN: (*To* VICKEY) See if we have any Polish tea.

(VICKEY *exits into kitchen.*)

MAUREEN: Mr Gallagher—

JONATHAN: Call me John.

MAUREEN: Where are your folks? Are they gonna come down?

JONATHAN: I handle the family affairs. All of em.

MAUREEN: All right then, let's sit.

(JONATHAN *and* MAUREEN *sit at dining table.*)

MAUREEN: Let's start with Dr Fleming.

JONATHAN: You're condescending.

MAUREEN: How old are you?

JONATHAN: Twenty-five.

MAUREEN: I'm twenty-seven—Dr Fleming, please?

JONATHAN: Dr Fleming was guardian to me, Kyle, Vickey, and our Ma and Pa.

MAUREEN: And what are their names?

JONATHAN: Marjorie and Phillip.

MAUREEN: (*Reading*) They're not your brother and sister.

JONATHAN: Probably not.

MAUREEN: They're listed as dependents.

JONATHAN: We all are. Margie and Phil are retarded.

MAUREEN: John, isn't it about time we cut out the jokes? You are joking?

JONATHAN: You didn't know?

MAUREEN: You said they're your parents.

(JONATHAN *nods.*)

MAUREEN: That's impossible.

JONATHAN: No, it's true.

MAUREEN: You're serious?

JONATHAN: Yes.

MAUREEN: Who are we talking about?

JONATHAN: What?

MAUREEN: Who's *challenged* here?

JONATHAN: Well, we're all—

MAUREEN: You know what I mean.

JONATHAN: Margie, Phil and Kyle.

MAUREEN: Falsifying claims and impersonating a licensed medical doctor is a serious crime.

JONATHAN: Can I be honest with you?

MAUREEN: *Can* you?

JONATHAN: I was hoping I'd never get caught. *(Then)* There's another phone in the kitchen if that one's not private enough.

MAUREEN: Will you stop anticipating every move that I make? *(She crosses to the kitchen door, hesitates.)*

JONATHAN: What?

MAUREEN: I'm feeling like I should know what to do. My supervisor is going to ask my assessment of this situation and a protocol and I honestly can't think of one.

JONATHAN: I can't imagine you get these assignments way out in the middle of nowhere if you're in their good graces.

MAUREEN: They say I have a mouth.

JONATHAN: No!

MAUREEN: I've been keeping it in check.

JONATHAN: I'll call them for you. I'll straighten the whole thing out, get ya outta here just like that. *(Snaps his fingers)* I know how to talk to those people.

MAUREEN: I'll bet you do.

MAUREEN exits into the kitchen. VICKEY re-enters, picks up phone receiver and covers the mouthpiece with her hand.

JONATHAN: No, Vickey.

VICKEY: It's our phone.

JONATHAN: Get away from there.

VICKEY: *(Whispering)* What's she want?

JONATHAN: Don't know yet. I think she's just taking some kind of survey or something.

VICKEY: She's nice.

(Off JONATHAN'*s look:)*

VICKEY: For a social worker. She's a lot prettier than the last one who came by.

JONATHAN: Well, she's not as pretty as you.

VICKEY: Cut it out. I don't think about stuff like that. That's boy stuff an' I ain't interested in boys.

JONATHAN: Bobby?

VICKEY: *(Flushed and disarmed)* Who told you about Bobby?!

JONATHAN: Nobody—except you—the way you talk about him—your voice gets a little sing-songy when he comes up.

VICKEY: He catches more crawdaddies than anybody. *(Changing her tone)* It ain't him, he's just a pal—who I'm really interested in is—a mystery. *(Evading)* What's she saying on the phone? We shoulda hid so she woulda left.

JONATHAN: And miss Jeb Sayer dancing up the trail on one leg?

*(*MAUREEN *re-enters. Beat.* VICKEY *crosses into kitchen and out.)*

JONATHAN: *(Continuing; to* MAUREEN*)* You look concerned.

MAUREEN: Do me a favor, John, be quiet so I can think.

JONATHAN: You're condescending again.

MAUREEN: Was I?

JONATHAN: Do you do that so you won't get to know me? That would throw social workers off their game, wouldn't it? Getting to actually know they're clients.

MAUREEN: *You* look concerned.

JONATHAN: *(He is)* Should I be?

MAUREEN: You have to return the money we've sent you for the past two years and they want to terminate your claim.

JONATHAN: What?!

MAUREEN: Your claim is fraudulent, you're not Dr Fleming.

JONATHAN: We need the money just as much now as when Fleming was alive. And if they cut us off, how will we live? You know I don't have the money.

MAUREEN: They want to see you in Richmond.

JONATHAN: Who?

MAUREEN: The state police. *(Then)* I'm just kidding, John. Doctors—you and your whole family.

JONATHAN: Then what?

MAUREEN: You don't have the right to ask "then what?" You forfeited that when you forged your guardian's signature and took funds from the state illegally. *(Beat)* They want assessments, physical and mental. I'll have to redo your file from the ground up. I am here to help you, Mr Gallagher, I'll do as much as I can, the state is on your side.

JONATHAN: What just happened to you?

(VICKEY enters with tea and cups.)

MAUREEN: Thank you, Vickey. Jonathan and I have some very important things to discuss and—

JONATHAN: We share everything that goes on about our family.

MAUREEN: All right.

(VICKEY *sits*.)

MAUREEN: Let's start with vital statistics.

JONATHAN: Phillip Lawrence and Marjorie Samantha Gallagher. Forty-seven and forty-five years old.

MAUREEN: What's their IQ?

JONATHAN: Dr Fleming always said they're both around sixty-five.

MAUREEN: Classically speaking, mildly retarded—

VICKEY: Retarded is retarded—that's what Johnny says.

JONATHAN: Kyle Theodore—fifteen—IQ of about fifty. Victoria Elizabeth—thirteen—about one hundred and ten. And I'm twenty-five and you're twenty-seven. My IQ is about hundred fifty-seven.

MAUREEN: One hundred and seven.

JONATHAN: One hundred fifty-seven.

MAUREEN: Do you know what that makes you?

JONATHAN: Odd. (*Then*) Don't believe me, ask the University of Virginia.

MAUREEN: You shouldn't be here.

JONATHAN: Since Dr Fleming died—

MAUREEN: Did you graduate?

JONATHAN: Almost. I need half a semester. Maybe a full year now that I've been gone for two years.

MAUREEN: Teaming up with qualified caregivers would have enabled you to complete your degree.

JONATHAN: I got my degree. I'm getting it every day.

MAUREEN: Changes are in order, John.

JONATHAN: You're not going to change anything.

MAUREEN: Are you threatening me?

JONATHAN: I'm letting you know my feelings.

MAUREEN: My feelings are that you are a criminal. That you have broken the law and that I could have you arrested. My feeling is that the individuals in this household are not receiving the proper care and I'm not sure, even under the sponsorship of the deceased Dr Fleming that you ever received what the State of Virginia would ever consider adequate stewardship. My feeling is that you have no power right now unless you want to make it physical. My feeling is that you don't belong here.

JONATHAN: I belong with my family.

MAUREEN: You belong where I say you belong.

JONATHAN: That's where you're wrong, Maureen, we all belong here. This is where we live. It's our home.

MAUREEN: You can't give them what they need.

JONATHAN: Yeah, I can.

MAUREEN: They can't give you what you need.

JONATHAN: I'm twenty-four years old, I'm a grown man, I decide what I need.

MAUREEN: You're a boy who's scared of the big bad world.

JONATHAN: I've seen those institutions, I know what they're like. No one is institutionalizing anyone in this house. This is my family, my home, my life.

MAUREEN: You've lied to us, you've defrauded us, you've taken upon yourself the responsibility of caring for people you're not equipped to take care of.

JONATHAN: I am more fit than a staff of clones in white jackets in a cold, dank gray building prescribing sedatives to keep everyone calm, quiet and inhumanly under control.

(Beat)

MAUREEN: And you call this Shangri-La?

JONATHAN: It is to us. You, too, if you'll let us show you.

MAUREEN: I'm open to anything you want to show me.

JONATHAN: You can turn off that social worker button?

MAUREEN: Try me. *(She crosses to the television, newly alarmed.)* This is brand new, where'd you get it?

JONATHAN: The people in town give us what we want that we can't afford on public assistance—food, clothes, hardware—

VICKEY: I threw a vase through the last one. You shoulda seen it spark, it was like the Fourth of July!

MAUREEN: Why do they do this for you?

JONATHAN: To keep us out of sight. They think I'll put Kyle, Margie and Phil in the town square, in raggedy clothes and dirty faces, and have them panhandle and pester all the tourists.

MAUREEN: Why do they think that?

JONATHAN: Cause that's what I told them.

MAUREEN: The outside world really does need to get a taste of you.

VICKEY: You must be *exhausted*, Miss Jankowski. Wouldn't you like to come with me to the creek and chill out? It's real nice and quiet.

JONATHAN: I'll fix supper while you're gone.

MAUREEN: I really can't stay.

JONATHAN: You think we'll poison you way back here in the woods and bury you under the wood pile? We only do that with the IRS. C'mon.

MAUREEN: First, you can't wait to get rid of me, now—

JONATHAN: I'll prove to you that I'm fit to take care of them. There's nothing I can't do. Vickey, get Miss Jankowski one of your T-shirts. She's staying.

(VICKEY *exits upstairs.*)

JONATHAN: I know I can be frustrating.

MAUREEN: You can be many things.

JONATHAN: I was out there for three years. I mean, if Charlottesville is considered a small town in this microcosm of existence we call our universe, then you can have the rest of it. I don't need it, I don't want it.

MAUREEN: You were home schooled.

JONATHAN: Sure, I was home schooled. But the good doctor was a brilliant man, so the tests say I'm brilliant. It didn't stop my classmates from staring, pointing fingers, laughing, looking at me funny—

MAUREEN: Why would they look at you funny?

JONATHAN: (*Shrugs*) People find out who you are, where you come from, who your folks are. Nobody can look after Phil, Margie and Kyle the way I do.

MAUREEN: You won't be abandoning Phil, Margie and Kyle—

JONATHAN: And Vickey?

MAUREEN: Maybe—

JONATHAN: Maybe's not good enough.

MAUREEN: They have special needs.

JONATHAN: We all have special needs.

(VICKEY *returns.*)

VICKEY: *(To* MAUREEN*)* Ready?

MAUREEN: Sure.

JONATHAN: What are Margie and Phil doing?

VICKEY: Screwin'—*around.* C'mon, Miss Jankowski.

(MAUREEN *and* VICKEY *exit through front door.)*

JONATHAN: *(Mostly to himself)* I'm fit.

(JONATHAN *gets a small bottle from cabinet, throws a pill into his mouth.* KYLE *enters, goes to TV, cannot turn it on.)*

JONATHAN: Kyle, what did I tell you about hugging strangers? You have to learn not to do that.

(KYLE, *barely listening, focuses on the TV.)*

KYLE: On! On!

(JONATHAN *turns it on with the remote control.* KYLE *gasps as the lights fade out.)*

(End of Scene 1)

Scene 2

(A small area downstage of the set is dimly lit. Perhaps there is the base of a tree, but it's not absolutely necessary. This is the bank of a creek or a small river. Off we hear MAUREEN *and* VICKEY.*)*

VICKEY: *(Off)* Come on!

MAUREEN: *(Off)* No, you go ahead.

VICKEY: *(Off)* Just hang your feet in, that's all I'm doing. C'mon, you'll feel a lot better.

MAUREEN: *(Off)* I feel fine. I'll just enjoy some of the fresh air here, I don't do this very often. It's so beautiful here. Hey, what are you doing? No, if you splash me I'm going to—Vickey, you had just better not!

(*Offstage we hear a splash.* VICKEY *and* MAUREEN *enter, drying themselves with towels.* MAUREEN *sits.*)

VICKEY: Now, don't you feel good? Don't the water make you feel good?

MAUREEN: The water makes me feel wet.

(VICKEY *laughs as* MAUREEN *lights a cigarette.*)

VICKEY: What's that like?

MAUREEN: What?

VICKEY: That.

MAUREEN: Cigarettes? They're okay, I like them, but only the low tars.

VICKEY: Can I try it?

MAUREEN: Have you ever smoked a cigarette before?

VICKEY: No, never, Johnny says they're no good.

MAUREEN: Listen to your brother, he's right.

VICKEY: How come you do it?

MAUREEN: I don't know, and I can't afford an analyst to find out.

VICKEY: I got a friend I usually go swimmin' with. Surprised they ain't here.

MAUREEN: What's her name?

VICKEY: It's a him. Bobby. Bobby Brown.

MAUREEN: Just you and him?

VICKEY: Sometimes. Y'know, he's only fifteen but his dad lets him make deliveries in their van. Sometimes we go for rides.

MAUREEN: What do you do?

VICKEY: Just mess around. How long you been doin' your job?

MAUREEN: Including my internship in college—about five years.

VICKEY: I still don't know what it is you do.

MAUREEN: Seems like all I do is drive. *(She picks a plant by the tree.)*

VICKEY: What is it?

MAUREEN: It's a fern. I had one at home but it died. They say you should talk to them.

VICKEY: Go on, say something to it.

MAUREEN: What do I call it?

VICKEY: It's name is—Fernie. And that's Mrs. Fernie.

MAUREEN: What do I say?

VICKEY: Tell them you're their social worker.

MAUREEN: Hello, Mr and Mrs Fernie, I'm Maureen and I'm your social worker.

VICKEY: Oh look, they're smiling. They sure are. What? They say they're glad to meet ya.

MAUREEN: Really?

VICKEY: Surely.

MAUREEN: I should carry them with me wherever I go then.

VICKEY: Oh—how come?

MAUREEN: I usually don't get many smiles.

VICKEY: Why?

MAUREEN: A lot of times the people I visit don't want my help, but if they weren't in trouble they wouldn't need it. It's difficult to make them see that sometimes.

VICKEY: I bet it's real excitin' to travel around so much. Most of the time all I get to do is go fishin' up in Hattiesburg or go crawdaddyin' in John's Creek.

Johnny did take me to Washington, DC one time, and I've been to Richmond a couple of times. Washington, DC was so exciting, I loved seein' all those statues of the presidents, specially the one of Mr Lincoln. There was sumthin' sad about ole Abe—melancholy, y'know? But I guess that's cause I know how he died—and the monument, you ever been up in the monument?

MAUREEN: Yes, you get a wonderful view of Washington, like you're above it all—like you're in an airplane.

VICKEY: Johnny and I were gonna walk up the stairs all the way to the top, all eight-hundred and somethin', but they were closed cause of vandalism—that's the way things go, huh? Johnny says he's gonna take me to New York and the Empire State Building and the World Trade Center—I like high places, the monument is the highest I ever been. I never been in a plane. I like to climb trees, too. Did you ever climb trees when you were little?

MAUREEN: I can't remember.

VICKEY: Well, I do. I spend a lot of time climbing trees, it's how I meditate and relax—I swim and then find a good tree and try my damndest to become one with nature, y'know, like David Carradine. I'm glad you came down here with me, Miss Jankowski.

MAUREEN: Call me Maureen.

VICKEY: Maureen—Johnny calls you Maureen sometimes. Do you think that we can be friends, Maureen?

MAUREEN: What would you call two people sitting under a tree, talking and enjoying the fresh air?

VICKEY: Does that mean yes.

MAUREEN: Yes.

VICKEY: This'll be a surprise for Johnny. He didn't think that you and me could be friends on account of social workers being trained to be cold and impersonal. Do they really train you to be like that?

MAUREEN: I like you, Vickey.

VICKEY: I like you, too, Maureen. Oh look, that fish is jumpin' clear out of the water, looks like a catfish to me—he musta got hold of one a them red peppers I threw down to the bottom last week. He's really jumping. You got a boyfriend?

MAUREEN: What brought that on?

VICKEY: I don't know. Do ya?

MAUREEN: I had a fiancee once, he asked me to decide between him and my job.

VICKEY: What happened? Oh.

MAUREEN: Do you have one?

VICKEY: Nah, just a pal.

MAUREEN: That's good. It's good to have pals. You're thirteen?

VICKEY: I'm thirteen now, but in a couple of weeks I'll be fourteen.

MAUREEN: You shouldn't come here alone.

VICKEY: I don't, it's usually—

MAUREEN: Not with Bobby.

VICKEY: How come? We'll see what Johnny says.

MAUREEN: Vickey, there are reasons for things. A lot of times you don't understand, but later you realize that someone was doing what's best—what's best for everyone. That's sort of what my job is. Do you know what I'm talking about?

VICKEY: Yeah.

MAUREEN: I'm going to get personal, Vickey, cause I think it's the kind of thing that just you and I could talk about in private. It's not why I came out here with you, bit since we're here—what do you know about biology?

VICKEY: I know I hate it, it's my worst class. Now anthropology—I'm good at that. That's what I'm gonna be when I grow up, an anthropologist.

MAUREEN: Has Jonathan told you anything about some of the things that happen to your body as you get older? Or maybe you've been taught some things in school.

VICKEY: I know a few things like that from Johnny and school. Why?

MAUREEN: Do you know about the menstruation cycle?

VICKEY: That's a Honda, ain't it?

MAUREEN: Do you know what it means for you as a growing woman?

VICKEY: Do you know that one time I caught a six-pound bass in this very creek? It's the biggest one to be pulled outta here in ten years. I got a trophy to prove it.

MAUREEN: You can have children. Have you begun menstruation, Vickey?

VICKEY: Why do you want to know? Did Johnny tell you?

MAUREEN: I know because you're a woman and it's time. How long?

VICKEY: Why are you asking me these questions? Friends don't ask each other "how long?" You ain't my friend, you're just a damn social worker, you're all alike, just like Johnny says. From now on you look in Dr Fleming's files for anything you want to know about me cause I'm through talkin, do you hear me, through! (*She runs off.*)

MAUREEN: Vickey! Vickey!

(MAUREEN *exits. Lights fade to black.*)

(*End of Scene 2*)

Scene 3

(Lights up on the dining and living room. MARGIE and PHIL are seated at the dining table. JONATHAN runs back and forth from the kitchen setting food and condiments on the table. VICKEY enters in a huff.

JONATHAN: Where's Miss Jankowski?

VICKEY: I ain't her baby-sitter.

JONATHAN: What happened?

VICKEY: (*Hands on hips*) I don't want to discuss it. She's a social worker. It was going all right, then—doggone it!

JONATHAN: Well, here, help set the table. I swear.

(MAUREEN *enters.*)

JONATHAN: Listen, I want to apologize for anything—

MAUREEN: I had a wonderful time, Vickey and I talked, we didn't get to finish, though.

VICKEY: We sure did, we talked plenty, we said everything that's gonna get said.

MAUREEN: There still are some questions I'd like to ask you, Vickey.

VICKEY: I told you what you could do with your questions.

JONATHAN: Whoa, whoa, wait a minute—Vickey, c'mon—

PHIL: Hiii!

MARGIE: Hi.

MAUREEN: Hi. I was beginning to think that John was hiding you from me.

MARGIE: We work real hard.

PHIL: Real hard.

MAUREEN: And what have you been working on, Marjorie?

MARGIE: Margie!

MAUREEN: Margie.

MARGIE: Pots.

JONATHAN: Everybody sit down—where's Kyle? (*He exits into kitchen.*)

MAUREEN: When he said supper, I thought he meant beans and franks. Just look at all this—mashed potatoes, peas and cauliflower, home-made rolls—Jello—

PHIL: Don't touch nuthin', we ain't s'posed to touch it.

MAUREEN: Why not?

MARGIE: Cause we ain't said the blessing yet.

VICKEY: We don't eat until we have thanked the Lord. Johnny says we got too much to be thankful for to let it go by.

MAUREEN: He's right—why don't I ever hear him say things?

VICKEY: Cause he says them to me, and Kyle, and Margie and Phil, and that's all!

(JONATHAN *enters from the kitchen and sets a roast on the table.* KYLE *enters through front door crying and grasping at his hair. In one hand is the deflated basketball.*)

VICKEY: Wha'dya do, try to eat it?

JONATHAN: Kyle, what is it?

(KYLE *shows him the basketball.*)

JONATHAN: It's got a hole in it.

(*This agitates* KYLE *more.*)

JONATHAN: Kyle? Kyle, will you listen, we can probably patch it.

MAUREEN: Let me try.

JONATHAN: I know how to handle my own brother.

MAUREEN: Well, you're not doing a very good job—move!

(MAUREEN *holds* KYLE *by the shoulders.*)

MAUREEN: Kyle, look at me, look at me, Kyle—look at me and listen—everything's going to be all right. Let me have the ball, Kyle?

(MAUREEN *slowly takes the ball from* KYLE *and passes it to* JONATHAN, *who shoves it away.*)

MAUREEN: Do you believe me when I say that, Kyle, huh?

KYLE: Yes, I b'lieve you, Reen.

MAUREEN: We're going to put it right under your chair so you won't be far from it.

KYLE: I love you, Reen.

MAUREEN: I love you, too, Kyle—let's eat, okay?

KYLE: I'm real hungry, Reen.

MAUREEN: Here, come sit next to me.

(*They sit.*)

JONATHAN: We're thankful, Lord, for the food we are about to receive and we're thankful for the health you've given us to enjoy it—thank you for watching over us and seeing us through another day. Don't stop watchin' over us and thank you for sending Miss Jankowski to visit with us. Amen.

ALL: Amen.

JONATHAN: Pass me your plate, Phil—Vickey, would you do Margie's? Maureen, help yourself, please.

MAUREEN: I'll help Kyle.

JONATHAN: That was real nice.

MAUREEN: I wasn't cold and impersonal?

(VICKEY *clears her throat.*)

MAUREEN: I noticed a swing out back, do you use it?

JONATHAN: That old tire?

MAUREEN: Those are the most fun—I used to um—there's a very interesting story Vickey might like to hear. My very first boyfriend had a tire swing in his backyard. I could talk him into pushing me for hours and he never got tired. I was twelve years old and I'd get up real high and kick my legs at the sun.

JONATHAN: Where was this, in Poland?

MAUREEN: The point being, Vickey, I suppose that was something like your climbing trees.

VICKEY: I can't tell ya how interesting that was.

JONATHAN: Where's your boyfriend now?

MAUREEN: When the swing broke, we broke up.

PHIL: Can I have another roll, please?

VICKEY: Here Phil, you're buttering it yourself this time.

PHIL: Okay.

KYLE: I want another roll.

MARGIE: You have a roll.

KYLE: I want another one!

VICKEY: Here! (*She slams a roll on* KYLE'*s plate.*)

JONATHAN: Vickey, take it easy. Here Phil, let me put the butter on it, you always make a mess.

MAUREEN: Does he have problems with motor functions like that?

JONATHAN: Yes, but he has no trouble molding clay.

MAUREEN: It probably has something to do with the sensation of the spinning, it stimulates certain nerves and adds to his coordination. It's not uncommon.

JONATHAN: Of course.

VICKEY: Huh!

JONATHAN: Quiet!

MAUREEN: This is very good!

JONATHAN: Dr Fleming made sure I knew how to cook. I guess he was looking ahead to when he wasn't around.

VICKEY: Poor Dr Fleming.

MAUREEN: What do you mean?

JONATHAN: She means that he's dead.

VICKEY: As a doornail.

JONATHAN: Kyle, do you want more potatoes?

KYLE: Yes.

VICKEY: Johnny?

JONATHAN: Yes?

VICKEY: When do I get my rollerskates?

JONATHAN: When do you want them?

VICKEY: How about right now?

JONATHAN: Do you think I'm a magician, do you think money grows on trees? Maybe I got em hanging out of my pockets, is that what you think? Billy Tucker brought a pair by while you were at the creek.

VICKEY: I don't believe you, where are they?

JONATHAN: They're in the kitchen, but finish your supper first.

VICKEY: I am finished. *(She exits into the kitchen.)*

MAUREEN: Margie—

MARGIE: You have to wait till I'm finished eatin', I don't talk with food in my mouth.

MAUREEN: Okay, I'll talk to Phil.

KYLE: Get serious, Phil.

MAUREEN: Phil, tell me about you and Margie.

PHIL: Margie?

MAUREEN: Yes, she's your wife, isn't she?

PHIL: We've been married for twenty-eight years.

MAUREEN: She's very pretty.

PHIL: Yeah. I like Margie. I like Margie—we have good sex.

(Off JONATHAN's *glare:)*

PHIL: Vickey said I could say that.

JONATHAN: Vickey!

*(*VICKEY *enters from the kitchen on skates.)*

VICKEY: He heard it on Mr Rogers' Neighborhood, it was one of his words for the day. He came out and he said, "Hi there boys and girls, our word for today is sex—sex—can you say sex? I think you can, uh-hm—" and then he started rubbin' himself, it was real disgustin'!

JONATHAN: I told you not talk that way in front of Phil, he always remembers.

VICKEY: There's no way he could forget that word. Look at me, I'm Linda Ronstadt and I'm gonna skate around the hills of Malibu overlooking the Pacific Ocean.

JONATHAN: Listen Linda, when you get to the ocean—keep goin'.

VICKEY: There's no oceans around here. I'm goin' down to the highway, it's the only flat surface.

JONATHAN: Be careful—be back before dark.

VICKEY: There's a box on the porch.

JONATHAN: What's in it?

VICKEY: Don't know, don't care. (*She skates off.*)

KYLE: I wanna go too—me?

JONATHAN: No, Kyle, you have to stay here and finish your supper.

MAUREEN: Kyle, don't you want to stay here and talk to me? I want to talk with you, and your brother, and your ma and pa.

KYLE: Dr Fleming?

JONATHAN: He doesn't understand completely.

KYLE: I do.

JONATHAN: He thought Dr Fleming was his dad.

MAUREEN: I wish I'd had a chance to meet him before he passed on. It's really remarkable what he's—

(*They all stare at* MAUREEN.)

MAUREEN: Do uh—Margie and Phil have sex often?

(JONATHAN *nearly chokes.*)

JONATHAN: Well, I uhh—don't know.

MAUREEN: You must have some idea.

JONATHAN: Well yes, I mean—springs, y'know—they make uhhh—coils.

MAUREEN: What about contraception?

(*Pause*)

PHIL: Rubbers.

(JONATHAN *buries his head in his hands.*)

MAUREEN: I see— (*To* PHIL) Why am I talking to him?

PHIL: I don't know.

MARGIE: I'm finished!

JONATHAN: Margie, where are your manners?

MARGIE: I'm finished!

(KYLE *laughs.*)

PHIL: Finish your peas.

MARGIE: I don't want em.

PHIL: She ain't finished her peas.

JONATHAN: Margie, I didn't give you very many, finish your peas, okay?

(MARGIE *purposely turns her plate over.*)

KYLE: She's finished.

MAUREEN: Now that wasn't very nice, Margie.

MARGIE: I don't care!

PHIL: God, she's a bitch tonight!

JONATHAN: Phil!

KYLE: Phil!

PHIL: Bitch, bitch, bitch!

MARGIE: Shut up!

JONATHAN: Both of you shut up!

KYLE: Both of you shut up!

MAUREEN: Jonathan?

JONATHAN: Now listen, damn it, don't make me mad, you two!

KYLE: Now listen, damn it—

(JONATHAN *eyes* KYLE *sharply.*)

JONATHAN: Damn that girl, I told her not to say words like that in front of them. I'm going to have to punish her.

KYLE: Dr Fleming?

JONATHAN: No, not Dr Fleming, and if you say his name one more time I'm going to crack you! *(To* MARGIE*)* What's a matter, you don't like my cooking?

MARGIE: It sucks!

(MARGIE *and* PHIL *continue to bicker.*)

JONATHAN: All right, that's it!

MAUREEN: Jonathan?!

JONATHAN: You're just showin' off cause we got company.

(MARGIE *screams.* PHIL *screams.*)

JONATHAN: Out of here! Do you hear me?! Hey listen, you're not the only ones who can scream—aaauuughh! I've had it up to here with both of you—I'll outscream the both of you put together! You know why? Because you're driving me as crazy as you are! Do you wanna hear the sound of a man going crazy?

(JONATHAN *yells blindly at them, but stops suddenly. Everyone senses something, they quiet down.* JONATHAN *speaks in a calm voice.*)

JONATHAN: Supper is finished.

(MARGIE *and* PHIL *exit up the stairs.*)

JONATHAN: Kyle—upstairs.

KYLE: But—I didn't do nuthin'.

JONATHAN: Kyle—

KYLE: —Uhhh—uhhh—basketball—

JONATHAN: To hell with the basketball—

MAUREEN: Kyle, he doesn't mean it.

JONATHAN: Upstairs, Kyle.

(KYLE *exits. Its an uncomfortable moment.* MAUREEN *reaches into her purse, takes out pad and paper and writes.)*

JONATHAN: Please stop doing that.

MAUREEN: Uh-huh—

JONATHAN: That never happens.

MAUREEN: Clearly.

JONATHAN: Vickey—

MAUREEN: You can start by not putting the blame on Vickey—it's you.

JONATHAN: I'm fit to take care of my family, this kind of episode happens, it doesn't prove—

MAUREEN: I've had it up to here with your "this is my family" routine. You are not the only one who's got a family, there are millions of people in the world, and guess what? They've all got families. I wouldn't be surprised if there isn't a family living down the road, maybe even two, and this may shock you, but even I've got a family.

JONATHAN: I bet you see them whenever you want.

MAUREEN: Had. I had a family. My parents died a few years ago. One died and the other couldn't go on.

JONATHAN: Brothers? Sisters?

MAUREEN: Uncles, cousins, friends, people I'm close to.

JONATHAN: You plan their lives?

MAUREEN: No.

JONATHAN: So you only plan the lives of people you don't know?

MAUREEN: Regardless of how you see my function or my role, John, someone responsible needs to be in charge here.

JONATHAN: That's me.

MAUREEN: Someone who isn't throwing away his life. Someone who is dedicated to taking care of your family because that is what they're trained to do, not because they feel guilty.

JONATHAN: I think you're confused.

MAUREEN: No, you're the confused one. And why, I don't know. Certain distinct personality traits aside, you have a great deal of potential, John. I admire you. I admire your heart. I admire your love, your dedication, but—you should be living a life like the rest of us. A life even more fulfilling than the rest of us.

JONATHAN: Because of all those qualities you just listed? But I thought this was America, the land of the free. Ah, only if you think, feel, and see the world in a certain point of view, otherwise you are— *(Then)* You like me, don't you?

MAUREEN: Excuse me?

JONATHAN: Do you like me?

MAUREEN: Even if I did, it has no place in this conversation.

JONATHAN: But you do? I need to know that I can speak to you.

MAUREEN: We're speaking.

JONATHAN: I mean, really speak to each other.

MAUREEN: I thought we were—

JONATHAN: Margie, Phil and Kyle speak to each other. We—*converse*—

MAUREEN: And you want more than that. You want to know if there's a possibility for more than that. Even if there were, I'd tell you "no."

JONATHAN: Because you have to? Because you never break the rules?

MAUREEN: Because it would be stupid. And unprofessional. And impulsive. And—stupid.

(Beat)

JONATHAN: Why "had"? What happened to your family? What happened to your brother or sister—that you're avoiding talking about.

MAUREEN: You don't want to know.

JONATHAN: There you go telling me what I want.

MAUREEN: I had a sister Vicky's age. When my parents died she had a choice of staying with our aunt and uncle in Ohio or she could live with me. She chose me. I was working, earning enough money for the both of us, making it work. I loved her so much and I really thought I could raise her just as well as my aunt and uncle. I wasn't travelling so much then, but I had to leave her alone sometimes. I did everything I could, it was still neglect. If I had really been responsible, she'd still be alive today.

JONATHAN: I see where this is going.

MAUREEN: There was a park across the street from where we lived. I let her go there on her own. She was like Vickey, she needed room to grow—to play and everybody knew everybody. There was a guy who was always there, he lived in the neighborhood. I should have known he was autistic. All the signs were there, but he seemed normal enough. I'd never seen him be anything but—*normal*. Still, there were signs. He was my sister's friend. He'd come over and have a sandwich. Signs, signs, signs. I wasn't there one day, he was overtired, overstimulated, he had a violent tantrum and before anyone knew it she was dead. But it was my fault.

JONATHAN: So now you're locking up all the crazies.

MAUREEN: Protecting them from themselves and people like me who used to believe that love was the cure for all ills.

JONATHAN: No one's ill here.

MAUREEN: For his own good. Kyle—

JONATHAN: Kyle, *what?*

MAUREEN: *(Reading* JONATHAN*)* You tell me *Kyle, what?* Was there an accident?

JONATHAN: It was a hug. A hug! *(Then)* The mayor's seventeen year old son. He gave Kyle a softball. Kyle was so happy about it he hugged him. Nothing happened, but when Kyle hugs, he hugs, he squeezed the air out of him for a moment but that's all. I told everyone to stay away from us and we'd be fine. But that kid *had* to be nice to the little retard. That kid, that *football* player screamed bloody murder when Kyle wouldn't let go. They came up here and they threatened and I threatened right back. That's why they don't want us in town.

MAUREEN: That little town? You were at the University, John, didn't you love that? C'mon, University of Virginia at Charlottesville is a beautiful campus. There are marvelous scholars there. The medical school is one of the best in the country. Why didn't you relocate there? Bring your family where they'd be close by?

JONATHAN: First, Dr Fleming wouldn't allow it. Secondly, no institutions, third, once he was out of the way I couldn't afford it—and lastly, I just plain don't want to go back.

MAUREEN: Why? What are you so afraid of?

JONATHAN: Why do you care?

MAUREEN: I've given my reasons.

JONATHAN: Um-hm. *(Then)* Do you know what it's like to be appreciated? That everything about you is necessary and needed? That every single day you look at faces that say to you "Thank god, you're here". I supposed you don't get a lot of that.

MAUREEN: I'd say none.

JONATHAN: There's nothing like being loved unconditionally, the feeling of belonging, being wanted, appreciated—it's something worth having, Maureen, something worth wanting—its something you can have here.

MAUREEN: You mean you?

JONATHAN: I mean you. It's what you want, isn't it? My guess is its why you became a social worker.

MAUREEN: I want *someone* to know that I'm trying to do what's best. Nobody every says "Thanks for trying, Maureen". It's usually "what do you want here? when are you leaving?" My dad used to say, "Don't be wishy-washy, Maureen," y'know, "use your best judgment and you'll be fine," but the way he said it made me feel good—that I was okay. *Nobody* makes me feel okay.

JONATHAN: I think you're okay. Kyle thinks you're okay. I have a ma and pa and sister and brother I'm wiling to share. I can see how much you miss yours. They'll appreciate you. I'm sure I can teach Kyle to say, "Don't be wishy-washy, Reen."

(MAUREEN, *covering, writes in her notebook.*)

JONATHAN: Wow.

MAUREEN: What?

JONATHAN: You were actually here, now you're gone again. *(Then)* What are you writing?

MAUREEN: Nothing. I don't seem to be writing anything.

JONATHAN: I think that's a step forward. *(Beat)* Vickey said something about a box on the porch. *(He exits onto the porch. He returns with a cardboard box. Lifting items from the cardboard box—)* One slightly charred and broken cane, one severely melted prosthetic leg.

(MAUREEN examines the leg, tosses it back into the box, newly resolute.)

JONATHAN: I'm really sor—

MAUREEN: I'll try to keep you out of jail.

(As the words settle—)

MAUREEN: You forged federal documents. That's how you love your family? Commit a crime, get incarcerated so that the State has to take your family from you? *(Then)* You're very charming, clever, manipulative, you should go back to school and get your Juris Doctorate, you'd do very well.

JONATHAN: Would you like me then?

(MAUREEN now writes in her notebook with a purpose.)

MAUREEN: Bring Phil, Margie, Vicky and Kyle to Richmond next Thursday.

JONATHAN: Charlottesville's closer.

MAUREEN: My doctors are in Richmond.

JONATHAN: Then what?

MAUREEN: Then you will be examined.

JONATHAN: Will we all come back home?

MAUREEN: Would you appreciate that?

JONATHAN: Would you do that? Would you really do that?

MAUREEN: Do you have a car?

JONATHAN: I have a truck.

(MAUREEN *hands* JONATHAN *an appointment sheet.*)

MAUREEN: That's the address, the time, and the doctor to request. I think its time for me to leave.

(KYLE *enters from upstairs.*)

JONATHAN: Kyle, what do you want?

KYLE: I wanna say bye.

JONATHAN: C'mere.

(JONATHAN *whispers in* KYLE'S *ear.* KYLE *faces* MAUREEN.)

KYLE: Don't be wishy-washy, Reen.

(MAUREEN *can barely hide the fact that she's moved.* KYLE *hugs her. She warmly taps him on the back and he releases. She picks up the box from Jeb Sayer. She exits through front door, stopping just a second to look at* JONATHAN.)

JONATHAN: Thanks, Maureen.

(MAUREEN *exits. We hear the sound of her car pulling away.* JONATHAN *remains at the door until the car is out of earshot.*)

(*Lights to black.*)

END OF ACT ONE

ACT TWO

Scene 4

(Later that evening. A rainstorm brews outside. There are occasional bursts of thunder and lightning. A teapot whistles in the kitchen. JONATHAN comes down the stairs carrying a large book, behind him is VICKEY carrying a school book, then KYLE with his basketball, MARGIE follows carrying a large piece of paper and coloring chalk, PHIL brings up the rear. JONATHAN walks very forthright into the kitchen, the entire entourage follows in procession, the whistling stops, JONATHAN enters again with a cup of chocolate, followed silently, stoically by the others. PHIL has a cup of chocolate. JONATHAN stops at the base of the stairs, turns to face them.)

JONATHAN: Stop following me.

MARGIE: I don't wanna go.

JONATHAN: There's nothing to worry about.

MARGIE: I like it here. I won't like Richmond.

JONATHAN: Everybody, it's only for one day. We'll come home and everything'll be just the way it was.

VICKEY: That's not what I heard. I learned a new word on Mr Rogers today—IN-CAR-CER-ATION. That means they lock you up in the hoosegow. See Johnny, in this twisted little Dr Fleming affair you broke the law at least once, and actually more we know about. Granted, it was on account of yours truly and cohorts, but just the same you're a wanted man. But the Feds know that if they came after you way back here in the hollers that we'd all disappear into the hills and it would cost them a fortune to find us. You're gonna walk right into their trap and it won't cost them nothin'.

JONATHAN: That's not funny, Vickey.

(MARGIE *cries loudly.*)

JONATHAN: What is it, Margie?

MARGIE: I don't want to go!

JONATHAN: You have work to do. You too, Phil. Let's focus on the Renaissance Fair, let me worry about everything else.

VICKEY: Maybe—maybe she got caught in the storm and got washed all the way to Tennessee.

(JONATHAN *considers this, exiting up the stairs, VICKY settles at the dining table. MARGIE sits in a chair, draws. PHIL looks over her shoulder sipping chocolate noisily.*)

VICKEY: Everybody be quiet, I gotta study.

(KYLE *goes into kitchen, returns with a large round apple basket, sets it on the floor, takes aim with the basketball.*)

KYLE: Watch this.

VICKEY: Bounce it.

KYLE: Watch this, watch this. (*He takes a shot by bouncing the basketball.*) I missed.

PHIL: (*To MARGIE*) Wrong color.

MARGIE: Who told you? I didn't hear Vickey. Who told you? Shut up.

PHIL: It's the wrong—

MARGIE: Shut up!

PHIL: It's—

MARGIE: Shut up!

VICKEY: Both of you shut up.

KYLE: Both of you shut up.

MARGIE: *(To* PHIL*)* Give it to me!

PHIL: *(Sing-song)* Margie, Margie, Margie—

KYLE: Watch this. *(He takes another shot.)*

MARGIE: *(To* PHIL*)* Give it to me!

PHIL: I'll do it.

MARGIE: Give it to me!

PHIL: I know what's pretty—you don't.

MARGIE: Piss on you, Phillip.

VICKEY: I can't study!

MARGIE: *(To* PHIL*)* Piss on you!

VICKEY: I'm warning you! I won't even be able to tell ya what I'm gonna do.

PHIL: What? Show me.

KYLE: Watch this—

VICKEY: *(To* KYLE*)* You haven't made a shot all week!

PHIL: *(To* VICKEY*)* Show me!

*(*VICKEY *looks up at* PHIL, *then at* MARGIE.*)*

VICKEY: John-ny!

PHIL: You're a kid.

VICKEY: John-ny!

KYLE: Watch this—John-ny!

PHIL: John-ny!

VICKEY: John-ny, I'm gonna kill him!

*(*JONATHAN *enters.)*

VICKEY: They're fighting and I can't study. It's raining and I can't go outside.

MARGIE: It wasn't me.

VICKEY: *(To* MARGIE*)* You're gonna go to hell.

JONATHAN: Who started it?

(MARGIE *shows* JONATHAN *the drawing.)*

MARGIE: He don't like this.

JONATHAN: At the Renaissance Fair, if somebody doesn't like something, are you going to piss on them?

MARGIE: I didn't say that.

JONATHAN: I heard you.

MARGIE: He took my color.

JONATHAN: *(To* PHIL*)* Give it back.

PHIL: I did.

VICKEY: *(To* JONATHAN*)* What did you find out?

JONATHAN: That we have to do just about anything she says. Never mind about that. Margie, Phil, cooperate with each other. This'll be your last pot before the fair, let it be your summum bonum.

VICKEY: What kind of bone?

JONATHAN: Summum bonum. It's Latin. It means all that is good—Phil's masterpiece.

KYLE: Watch this. *(He makes the shot.)*

JONATHAN: Two points!

(KYLE *gives* JONATHAN *the basketball.)*

KYLE: Dunk.

JONATHAN: C'mon, Kyle.

KYLE: Dunk!

JONATHAN: Well—

(JONATHAN *stuffs the ball into the basket. He and* KYLEY *slap fives.)*

JONATHAN: Any more chocolate?

VICKEY: In the kitchen.

JONATHAN: *(To* MARGIE*)* No fighting.

(JONATHAN *exits into kitchen.* MARGIE *marches up the stairs.)*

VICKEY: Margie's just your match, Phil.

PHIL: I got tired of arguin'.

VICKEY: That's why she wins all your fights.

PHIL: I got tired.

VICKEY: She don't get tired. Don't start nuthin' when we go to the Renaissance Fair, she'll yell and scream and Johnny'll get nervous and crash through a guardrail and our insides'll be painted all over the Blue Ridge mountains.

PHIL: She don't win all the time.

VICKEY: She sure does.

PHIL: I get tired. What's that?

VICKEY: Geography.

PHIL: Is that Brazil?

VICKEY: Yep.

PHIL: Margie don't know what pretty is. She wants to tell me what color's pretty.

VICKEY: Do you mind?

PHIL: Want some chocolate?

VICKEY: No, thanks.

PHIL: I'll make you some.

VICKEY: No, thanks, you just sit there and look like Argentina.

PHIL: I like Brazil.

VICKEY: Then look like Brazil.

(JONATHAN *enters.*)

JONATHAN: About time for everyone to go to bed.

PHIL: I don't wanna sleep with Margie.

JONATHAN: That's a switch.

PHIL: Will they buy our pots, John?

JONATHAN: Sure.

PHIL: Will they? I don't work so hard fer nuthin.

JONATHAN: It doesn't matter if you sell them, it's the effort that counts.

PHIL: Is that the way business works?

JONATHAN: Well—

PHIL: We got a product.

JONATHAN: Yes.

PHIL: You said that.

JONATHAN: I did say that.

PHIL: We'll make money.

JONATHAN: Not necessarily.

PHIL: Why make em?!

JONATHAN: You're making them because—

PHIL: Cause you say so.

JONATHAN: Not because I say so.

PHIL: Who wants em? Who needs em?

(*There is anxious knocking at the front door.* KYLE *rushes to the door and opens it.* MAUREEN *walks in drenched.*)

KYLE: Hi, Reen!

MARGIE: Hi, Kyle. *(To* JONATHAN*)* My car broke down. It's raining buckets out there. If it weren't for some kid in a van giving me a ride I don't know what I would have done.

VICKEY: Hair to his shoulders, a big ol' gap between his two front teeth?

(Off MAUREEN*'s nod:)*

VICKEY: That must have been Bobby. Darn, did he go home already?

MAUREEN: Said to tell you he had chores he had to tend to.

VICKEY: And I guess I got homework.

*(*JONATHAN *goes into kitchen.* VICKEY *and* PHIL *exit upstairs.* MAUREEN *is left alone on stage, wondering.)*

MAUREEN: John?

JONATHAN: *(Off)* What?

MAUREEN: What are you doing?

JONATHAN: Making some hot chocolate to warm you up.

*(*PHIL *returns with a towel.)*

PHIL: *(To* MAUREEN*)* Sit.

*(*MAUREEN *sits.* PHIL *dries her hair with the towel.* VICKEY *returns with a blanket, she wraps it around* MAUREEN*.)*

MAUREEN: Thank you. *(To* JONATHAN*, off)* Can you give me a lift to the hotel?

*(*JONATHAN *returns with a steaming cup of chocolate. Gives it to* MAUREEN*.)*

JONATHAN: Not in this rain. You should get out of those wet clothes. Are you hungry?

MAUREEN: No.

JONATHAN: Tired?

MAUREEN: Very.

JONATHAN: You take my bed, I'll take some blankets and a pillow and sleep down here on the sofa.

MAUREEN: I can't do that.

JONATHAN: All right, you sleep on the sofa. We have some dry clothes that should fit you. How about some biscuits? Phil, get her some biscuits. *(To* MAUREEN*)* Just to snack on.

(PHIL *exits into the kitchen.)*

MAUREEN: My car stalled. I killed the battery trying to restart it. It was raining so hard I couldn't see two feet in front of me. This is the blackest night I think I've ever seen. Do you have booster cables?

JONATHAN: Fresh out.

MAUREEN: Well, once I get to the hotel I can call a serviceman.

JONATHAN: It's silly to go out in this rain.

KYLE: Reen, watch!

KYLE takes a shot with the basketball.

MAUREEN: Very nice, Kyle. *(To* JONATHAN*)* You're not going to help me get to the hotel?

VICKEY: Why didn't you ask Bobby? He'd drive you to Richmond if you asked him. He knows every back road there is from here to Mississippi.

JONATHAN: And he's only fourteen.

MAUREEN: I'm glad I didn't ask.

JONATHAN: I'll take you when the rain let's up.

MAUREEN: If.

JONATHAN: If there's nothing else we can do to make you comfortable, don't mind me if I read, I'm a couple of weeks behind in my journals.

(JONATHAN *sits in a chair, reading, rapidly turning the pages.* MAUREEN *strolls toward* VICKEY, *whose face is buried in her textbook.)*

MAUREEN: I love geography.

VICKEY: Meanin' you're good at it?

MAUREEN: Try me.

VICKEY: What's the highest mountain range in South America?

MAUREEN: The Andes.

VICKEY: What's the capitol of Buenos Aires—I mean, Argentina—skip that one—what's the capitol of— what's the longest river?

MAUREEN: The Amazon.

VICKEY: I didn't say South America.

MAUREEN: The Nile. What's the capitol of Uruguay?

VICKEY: Montevideo.

MAUREEN: You looked.

VICKEY: I did not.

MAUREEN: Close the book.

VICKEY: You're saying I cheated. Well, I don't need to answer somebody who doesn't trust me. I'll study by myself. You know what you are?

MAUREEN: What?

VICKEY: Competitive.

(PHIL *enters with a plate of biscuits.* MAUREEN *takes one.)*

VICKEY: She's just like all the rest, ain't she, Johnny?

JONATHAN: Uh-huh. It's rainin' cats and dogs and coyotes, it's the middle of the night an all she can think about is gettin' away. Our couch ain't even good enough. It is ugly, though. Knew we should've got it re-upholstered last Fall.

VICKEY: Wouldn't make no difference, she just don't like us. *(Sighs)* Looks like I only have one friend— Bobby. He likes me cause I'm me. He doesn't ask a lot of questions.

MAUREEN: How do you know he's interested in you if he doesn't ask questions?

VICKEY: I can tell. I got a question. What would happen if I was pregnant?

JONATHAN: Vickey—

VICKEY: In biology class we were dissecting cats and I opened one up and she was fulla kittens. It made me sad.

MAUREEN: Are you?

VICKEY: Fulla kittens? Nah. I got a B on my last test. I get A's in everything else. Well, almost A's. You want some honey? Here. I collected it myself. Had to fight off a whole swarm of bees, it was like the Little Big Horn, only I lived as opposed to you-know-who. I did get stung a coupla times.

PHIL: That's the color I want! That's it! *(He grabs* MAUREEN's *purse.)* She don't think of me—she don't—I get ideas.

MAUREEN: Of course you do, who says you don't?

PHIL: This is the color—I know this is my color—what do you think?

MAUREEN: I think—

PHIL: You and Margie—

MAUREEN: No, Phil, I—

PHIL: This is the color I want.

PHIL exits up the stairs, taking the purse with him.

JONATHAN: Phil!

MAUREEN: It's okay, it's empty. You taught me that.

(VICKEY *closes her book ceremoniously.*)

VICKEY: Done.

JONATHAN: Good night, Vickey.

VICKEY: G'night.

(VICKEY *exits.* JONATHAN *crosses to the window.*)

JONATHAN: (*In a spooky voice*) It's a terrible night. Lightning, rain, thunder—Dr Fleming died on a night like this. A night like this—you're lucky. It wouldn't be unlikely—a small car—it's dark—a strange road—you get washed into a ravine.

(KYLE *exits.*)

JONATHAN: It's good that you made your way back here.

MAUREEN: You're just trying to scare me, aren't you? Aren't you?

JONATHAN: Did your car really break down?

MAUREEN: Yes.

JONATHAN: So how far did you get?

MAUREEN: I pulled off at Henry's Vista where it looks out over the valley. I caught the sun just going down beneath the storm clouds. I sat there thinking, I don't know how long, and then it started pouring buckets.

JONATHAN: Thinking about what?

MAUREEN: What to do with you, how to get you into a place where you can realize what I see is an enormous amount of potential.

JONATHAN: What's wrong with just leaving me alone? I have everything I need. They love me, pass or fail.

MAUREEN: And that's enough?

JONATHAN: I've considered finishing school. I was top five in my class at UV. If I finished my science degree I could work anywhere. I dreamed of working in Washington, D.C., getting married, having a family. Then Dr Fleming died. I came home. Or I came home and he died, I don't remember. The house was run down since I left. He was old and was only interested in his research. I began fixing things. Simple things like doors coming off hinges. The pump on the well, the venting in the attic for the kiln. I started building a basketball court for Kyle. I never really had a plan, but a plan got hold of me. I realized I never really belonged at school, I was the most happy when I was home. We're all happy and safe here. That is until you came along. Maybe you coming here has nothing to do with why the State sent you here, maybe we're caught up in a plan that's bigger than that.

MAUREEN: A plan like you and I fall hopelessly in love like they do in fairy tales?

JONATHAN: Not hopelessly, we can never give up hope.

(MARGIE *enters from upstairs with a large white piece of construction paper.* PHIL *follows with several pieces of colored chalk.* VICKEY *and* KYLE *are behind them.* MARGIE *pushes aside whatever's on the dining table and lays the paper on it.*)

MARGIE: *(To* MAUREEN*)* Come here. I don't draw too good.

PHIL: Let me—

MARGIE: No! *(To* MAUREEN*)* I don't draw too good because—uh—because uh—you know.

MAUREEN: This is a—

MARGIE: For flowers? It's blue.

MAUREEN: Yes?

MARGIE: Watch. *(She draws with the chalk.)*

MARGIE: See?

(MAUREEN *makes a small addition with the chalk.)*

MARGIE: Yes—you're good.

PHIL makes his own drawing.

PHIL: The color of—Brazil.

PHIL compares the purse and the picture in VICKEY'S geography book.

MAUREEN: That's an earth tone.

PHIL: *(To* MARGIE*)* You don't know what pretty is.

MARGIE: *(To* MAUREEN*)* What do you think?

MAUREEN: They're both—they're both— *(To* JONATHAN*)* You could help.

MARGIE: Talk to me.

PHIL: Mine reaches up. Earth tones.

MARGIE: No.

PHIL: Earth tones. Yes?

MAUREEN: Make two.

(MARGIE *and* PHIL *turn to* JONATHAN.*)*

MARGIE: John?

MAUREEN: That one. Considering the shape of the vase as I interpret it from this—schematic. It seems to be reaching out, swirling, like a carousel spiraling up from Earth. *(Pointing to* PHIL*'s drawing)* Definitely that one.

(JONATHAN *examines the drawings. Referring to* MARGIE*'s drawing—)*

JONATHAN: Sky, it reaches up for the peacefulness and calm of the sky which is why she's got this shade of blue. *(To* PHIL*)* Margie designs em, you make em, why are you trying to change things?

PHIL: I have ideas. All the time. So many, so many you can't know.

JONATHAN: Margie designs em, you make em—that's teamwork.

PHIL: I design em, Margie makes em—that's teamwork, too.

VICKEY: I like Phil's.

PHIL: It's the color of Brazil—and trees.

MAUREEN: *(To* JONATHAN*)* Look at it objectively. Stop contradicting me.

JONATHAN: We're doing Margie's.

PHIL: Cause you say so?

JONATHAN: That's right.

PHIL: Give me some rest! Give me some rest! I—I—I—won't stay here.

JONATHAN: Phil, it's raining.

PHIL: They don't need my pots!

JONATHAN: People buy lots of things they don't need.

PHIL: They just gonna laugh at me.

JONATHAN: Let em laugh.

PHIL: I hate it. I won't—I won't. Give me some rest.

JONATHAN: Phil, it's a Renaissance Fair. You got a right to be there. You're gonna do business like they did in the sixteen hundreds. You set up shop and sell your wares.

PHIL: I want ta sell now, not then. I want business today. Can I—I—do I got the right—today? Can I? I'm leaving.

MARGIE: Who's gonna take care of you?

PHIL: I'll get a job.

MARGIE: Doin' what?

PHIL: I'll make things—I'll make pots! I'll take care of everybody. *(To* JONATHAN*)* You don't like my ideas?! You like em! I tell you! You! You my son! You like em!

MARGIE: Stop it! Stop it!

*(*MARGIE *tears up her drawing. She hugs* PHIL *for a long while. They exit upstairs.)*

KYLE: *(To* MAUREEN*)* Tell a story.

VICKEY: Kyle, she's the boogey woman, her stories will scare you.

KYLE: No, they won't. *(To* MAUREEN*)* Please? I'll love you if you do.

*(*KYLE *pulls* MAUREEN *onto the sofa.)*

MAUREEN: Which one?

KYLE: The old woman and the shoe—

MAUREEN: Really? Well, once upon a time there was an old woman who lived in a shoe, she had so many children she didn't know what to do— *(Stops)* Kyle, I'm sorry, this was never one of my favorites. How about—

JONATHAN: How about time to go to bed.

*(*KYLE *whines.)*

JONATHAN: Kyle?

*(*KYLE *collects himself, kisses* MAUREEN*.)*

KYLE: 'Night, 'Reen.

*(*KYLE *exits.* VICKEY *glances out the window.)*

VICKEY: It ain't never gonna stop rainin', it's gonna rain forever. *(She exits up the stairs.)*

JONATHAN: More chocolate?

MAUREEN: No—thanks. (*She notices the steel ball pendulum.*) I've seen these.

JONATHAN: Newton's Cradle—inertia, mass, velocity and the transference of kinetic energy.

(*Off* MAUREEN's *look:*)

JONATHAN: In simpler terms, for every action there's an equal and opposite reaction.

(MAUREEN *sets the balls in motion, CLICK-CLACK, CLICK-CLACK.*)

MAUREEN: How long will it do this?

JONATHAN: For a while. Friction and resistance make it stop.

MAUREEN: Air.

JONATHAN: Right, that kind of resistance.

(JONATHAN *steps close to* MAUREEN, *kisses her, until the balls stop their motion.*)

MAUREEN: I must be the worst social worker ever.

JONATHAN: A good kisser, though.

(MAUREEN *kisses* JONATHAN *again, as if to answer a question. She pulls away, putting space between them.*)

JONATHAN: Friction and resistance.

MAUREEN: We're both lonely, Jonathan. That's all that's going on here.

JONATHAN: I'm not—

MAUREEN: You know what I mean. We're both consumed by our duties to the point that—listen, I should check in. I need to inform my supervisor that I'm a day behind.

(*From off,* PHIL *and* MARGIE *begin to bicker loudly.*)

JONATHAN: Use that phone. I'll be right back.

(JONATHAN *exits up the stairs.* MAUREEN *dials.*)

MAUREEN: Hi. This is Jankowski. I'm at the Gallagher home. I got caught in a rainstorm, I'm running about a day behind. I won't get to the Smith triplets until tomorrow afternoon. Yes, a day. Listen, do you know what sunshine is? Do you know how it works, how it facilitates travel when I go this deep into the field? Now, do you understand how rain has kind of the opposite effect as sunshine? Okay. Yes. As soon as I can. But listen, the situation we discussed—we have field doctors, why do these people have to come to Richmond? They seem to be under control. Really? And that's why? Is that an order?

(MAUREEN *hangs up.* JONATHAN *returns.*)

JONATHAN: (*Re* MARGIE *and* PHIL) Creative differences.

MAUREEN: I have to go.

JONATHAN: What did they say to you?

MAUREEN: They were concerned about the children.

JONATHAN: Vickey's enrolled in the public school system here, she's in perfect health, full vaccinations, that goes for everyone. I work with Kyle every single day on comprehension and learning, no one could give him more than I'm giving him.

MAUREEN: Vickey's at puberty.

JONATHAN: Even our dirtwater school district has sex education and what they don't tell her I do.

MAUREEN: And for Ob/Gyn?

JONATHAN: I take her to a midwife.

MAUREEN: A midwife?

JONATHAN: If something's wrong, the midwife will tell me and we'll go to Charlottesville or Richmond and get it taken care of.

MAUREEN: I suppose you counsel Margie and Phil on contraception?

JONATHAN: They don't need it, they know what they're doing.

MAUREEN: You leave it up to them?

JONATHAN: I don't referee the wrestling match, if that's what you're asking.

MAUREEN: What if one day Margie wakes up one day and—

JONATHAN: *(Calling off)* Margie! Get down here!

(MARGIE *enters.)*

MARGIE: What?

JONATHAN: Do you want more children?

MARGIE: No, it hurt me. It hurt me real bad. You ain't gonna make me, are you?

(MARGIE *clings to* JONATHAN.)

MARGIE: Johnny, don't let her make me. Make her leave me alone.

JONATHAN: Nobody's gonna do anything to you.

(PHIL *steps into view on the stairs.)*

PHIL: Son?

JONATHAN: You like that, don't ya?

PHIL: What?

JONATHAN: Calling me son.

PHIL: Yeah.

JONATHAN: *(To* MAUREEN*)* Satisfied?

(PHIL *takes* MARGIE's *hand.)*

PHIL: We have work to do, sweetie.

(PHIL *and* MARGIE *exit.)*

MAUREEN: There's no discussing this with you, is there?

JONATHAN: If it ain't broke, don't fix it.

(Beat)

MAUREEN: You want your family, I want them to see a real doctor.

JONATHAN: Then what?

MAUREEN: Then I'll file a petition for change of guardianship into your name.

JONATHAN: Really?

MAUREEN: Really.

(JONATHAN hugs MAUREEN warmly. She taps him on the back and he releases.)

JONATHAN: And—

MAUREEN: There is no "and". (She crosses to window.) The rain's stopped. Would you take me to the hotel now, please, Mr Gallagher?

JONATHAN: Don't do that.

MAUREEN: Don't give me orders!

JONATHAN: I'm sorry.

MAUREEN: No, I'm sorry. Can we go?

(JONATHAN and MAUREEN exit.)

(Lights to black)

(End of Scene 4)

Scene 5

(The day after the trip to Richmond, late afternoon. JONATHAN *enters through the front door carrying a bag of groceries and a cord of rope.)*

JONATHAN: I'm home!

*(*JONATHAN *sets the groceries on the table.* VICKEY *enters from upstairs and hugs* JONATHAN *dearly.* KYLE *enters from kitchen, scratching his groin.)*

JONATHAN: I thought you were all gonna sleep through the whole day. That trip to Richmond yesterday really wore everyone out,

VICKEY: I love you, Johnny.

JONATHAN: Well thanks, I sure didn't expect this.

VICKEY: That's not what you're supposed to say, you're supposed to say, "Vickey, I love you, too."

JONATHAN: Vickey, I love you, too.

VICKEY: And now you're supposed to hug me again.

*(*JONATHAN *hugs* VICKEY.*)*

VICKEY: Oh Rhett, I was so worried you were captured, or even worse, killed by those northerners who are settin' fire to our way of life.

KYLE: I love you, too, Jonathan.

JONATHAN: And I love you, Kyle.

*(*KYLE *hugs* JONATHAN.*)*

KYLE: Oh Rhett!

*(*JONATHAN *hands* KYLE *the groceries.)*

JONATHAN: *(To* KYLE*)* Put the groceries away, Scarlet.

*(*KYLE *exits into the kitchen with the bags of groceries.)*

VICKEY: Look, I know you're all lovesick over Miss Jankowski, but are you so heartbroken you're gonna hang yourself?

JONATHAN: It's to tie down the boxes. I got the license for the fair.

VICKEY: Really?! All right!

JONATHAN: She didn't call?

VICKEY: Jeez, maybe you should hang yourself. (*She rubs her stomach gingerly.*)

JONATHAN: You okay?

VICKEY: It's just a cramp. I'm fine. I'm really fine. I'm growing up really fast.

JONATHAN: Look, think you could keep them quiet for me tonight? And you could finish your book or something?

VICKEY: Sure.

JONATHAN: What are you reading?

VICKEY: It's about people an stuff.

JONATHAN: What kinda people an stuff?

VICKEY: South Americans…what they do to em when they don't want em gettin' pregnant…stuff like that.

JONATHAN: What do they do?

VICKEY: Well, in Bogota…

JONATHAN: Bogota…it's pronounced Bogota.

VICKEY: Well…there, they send all the peasants to get checkups and they fix em.

JONATHAN: Who sends them?

VICKEY: The government.

JONATHAN: Lucky thing we're not in Bogota. Look, you think you could do that for me?

VICKEY: Why don't you go to a movie or somethin' if you want quiet?

JONATHAN: It can be quiet here.

VICKEY: Just wait till…

JONATHAN: I don't have to leave my house to get quiet!

VICKEY: Y'know, ever since…

JONATHAN: Don't "ever since" me—

VICKEY: Why are you gettin' all huffy with me?! I ain't done nuthin' to you and I ain't your damned social worker. Maybe I have things to I'm worried about, but you're howling at the moon so much like a lovesick coyote you ain't got time.

(KYLE *enters.*)

KYLE: I—I—put the groceries up.

JONATHAN: Fine, Kyle. Great. Thanks. (*To* VICKEY) Why're you talking to me this way?

VICKEY: If you ain't gonna talk to me like we always been talking then I'm gonna talk this way. You been like this ever since Miss Jankowski came. And now ya come home all hunkered up an you won't tell nobody.

KYLE: Talk John.

JONATHAN: (*To* VICKEY) Well, Miss Jankowski's not here and she's not going to be, so I hope you're finished.

KYLE: Talk John.

JONATHAN: Kyle, knock it off. I just wanted some quiet—is that too much to ask?!

VICKEY: Somethin's buggin' you and I wanna know about it.

KYLE: Tell us about it, Johnny.

JONATHAN: Kyle, quit tellin' me what to do. *(To* VICKEY*)* I didn't get all our costumes.

VICKEY: Big deal.

JONATHAN: Mr Wainwright was supposed to have em ready today. Kyle's was the wrong size. I wouldn't take them. He said he'd try to get one before Sunday. The fair starts tomorrow!

VICKEY: Johnny, calm down. You know you can't get too excited.

KYLE: Calm down, Johnny—tell us about it!

*(*JONATHAN *slaps* KYLE. KYLE *stands mute.)*

VICKEY: It's enough other people doin' stuff to em— you don't have to go pickin' on em.

JONATHAN: I'm sorry, Kyle, I didn't mean to hit ya. Forgive me?

KYLE: No.

JONATHAN: I want you to slap me back, Kyle. Okay?

KYLE: 'Kay.

JONATHAN: I slapped you, so you have the right to slap me. All right?

KYLE: 'Right.

*(*JONATHAN *points to his cheek.)*

JONATHAN: Right here. Now, not too hard, all right?

*(*KYLE *slaps the dickens out of* JONATHAN*.)*

JONATHAN: That was good, Kyle. You want some ice cream?

KYLE: I wanna slap you again.

JONATHAN: No, I don't think so.

*(*MARGIE *enters through front door with flowers.)*

JONATHAN: *(Continuing; to* MARGIE*)* You think this is a country club, don't you? Everybody else works while you pick flowers.

MARGIE: Get off my back.

JONATHAN: We have a work schedule, remember? Margie, the first day of the Fair is tomorrow.

MARGIE: I don't care, I don't give a shit. I don't.

JONATHAN: Yes, you do. I know you do.

MARGIE: How do you know, hunh?! It's not your flesh. It's mine. It's mine! You don't know how I feel. What makes you think you know how I feel?! Who told you that?! I didn't. I didn't tell you so how do you think you know?

JONATHAN: I'm sorry.

MARGIE: You know what I know? Anybody can do whatever they want with me. You let them do whatever they want. That's what I know.

JONATHAN: They examined you, gave you a few shots.

MARGIE: I'm not a fool!

JONATHAN: *(To* VICKEY*)* You know what she's talking about?

VICKEY: *(Shrugs)* She don't like nobody but Phil touchin' her, I guess. Playin' with all that clay gives him magic fingers.

JONATHAN: Margie, I'll find out and then I'll tell ya.

MARGIE: You better cause I wanna know.

JONATHAN: I will.

MARGIE: I wanna know!

JONATHAN: Work.

MARGIE: I'm not foolin'! *(She exits upstairs.)*

VICKEY: I told ya it wasn't gonna be quiet around here. You yelled at us more the last week than the whole two years we been on our own.

(JONATHAN *stares out the window.*)

VICKEY: Earth to Johnny, Earth to Johnny. You'll get over it. They'll send somebody else.

JONATHAN: Vickey, you are so good to me.

VICKEY: You're my brother. *(Pause)* What would happen if I was pregnant?

JONATHAN: You'd probably have a baby. Why?

VICKEY: I just been thinking about it, that's all.

JONATHAN: By the way, I picked up some—

VICKEY: Sanitary napkins?

JONATHAN: Yeah. Maybe that's what's making you think about babies. Is it—are you—

VICKEY: Am I on my period?

JONATHAN: Yeah.

VICKEY: Yeah, I am. What are the odds my baby would be retarded.

JONATHAN: High.

VICKEY: Well then, I guess I shouldn't think about having children, that's a load off my mind.

JONATHAN: Just like that, huh?

VICKEY: Just like what, Johnny?

JONATHAN: Just like that—God, Vickey, if you think about it I wish you'd be serious.

VICKEY: Well God, if they're gonna come out retarded—they're a lot of trouble.

JONATHAN: Vickey, you just don't know, humans in general are a lot of trouble—you're a lot of trouble but I wouldn't give you up for anything in the world.

VICKEY: Do you really mean that?

JONATHAN: I really mean it. All you can hope for in this world is to be loved and to be able to love.

(JONATHAN *puts an arm around* KYLE *and squeezes.*)

JONATHAN: What's wrong with you, Kyle?

KYLE: I'm retarded.

JONATHAN: Who's screwing up the world?

KYLE: You.

JONATHAN: God, he learns fast.

VICKEY: I thought you were getting tired of us.

JONATHAN: Why would you think that? (*He picks up the rope.*)

VICKEY: Where ya goin'?

JONATHAN: The rope on the swing is frayed, I'm gonna replace it.

VICKEY: I swing on it all the time, there's nothing wrong with it.

(*The phone rings.* JONATHAN *rushes to answer it.*)

JONATHAN: Hello. Mr Wainwright. Okay, I'm listening. Okay. Well, good. I'm glad you feel that way. You better had. Mr Wainwright? What I meant to say was thanks. (*He hangs up.*) Kyle, they couldn't get a costume for you in time, so Mrs Wainwright is sewing one for you.

KYLE: She better had.

(JONATHAN *exits through the kitchen,* KYLE *follows.* VICKEY *rubs her stomach gingerly.* MARGIE *and* PHIL *enter from upstairs.* MARGIE *places a beautiful vase on the table and puts flowers in it.)*

VICKEY: That's pretty. We ought to be able to make a lot of money selling these if they're all like this. I'll be able to buy a roller-disco outfit.

PHIL: I want to get it for you.

VICKEY: Thanks, Daddy. *(She sits somewhere above it all, on top of a table, stand or bureau, cross-legged, contemplative. She lights a cigarette, savors a puff.)*

MARGIE: I'm hungry, I want supper.

PHIL: John's not here, Margie, we gotta wait for John.

MARGIE: I'm still hungry.

PHIL: I'll make supper.

MARGIE: You will?

PHIL: Yeah.

(Pause)

MARGIE: When, Phil?

PHIL: I'll make it—I'll make supper right now.

MARGIE: Right now?

PHIL: Yeah, right now.

MARGIE: Okay.

PHIL: Okay?

MARGIE: Okay.

PHIL: Supper?

MARGIE: Yes.

PHIL: Okay.

(PHIL exits into kitchen. MARGIE sits at the table and whistles to herself. She cries. He re-enters, trying to console her.)

MARGIE: Don't touch me! Don't touch me, Phillip! Don't!

PHIL: What's wrong? What's wrong?

MARGIE: Give me—give me—what did they do?! I can't—I can't—they don't know what I feel—I wish I could—I wish—I could think. I wanna think!

PHIL: Why?

(PHIL *caresses* MARGIE.)

PHIL: I'll make you something. You'll feel better, won'tcha? You're hungry, Margie.

(PHIL *exits.* MARGIE *tries to whistle, but can't. She and* VICKEY *are silent, aware of each other, both rocking to themselves. There is the sound of a car pulling up to the house. A knock at the door)*

VICKEY: Come on in, Bobby.

(MAUREEN *enters.)*

MAUREEN: I'm not Bobby.

VICKEY: Well, maybe y'are and then again, maybe y'aren't. Pepperidge Farm remembers. What do you want?

MAUREEN: Where's John?

VICKEY: Gone all day so there's no use you hangin' around. He's gone to get—our costumes, yeah, that's what he said—for the Renaissance Fair. We're gonna go and sell some pot.

MAUREEN: What?

VICKEY: Go and sell our pots—

(MAUREEN *crosses to* VICKEY, *hands out for the cigarette.)*

MAUREEN: Give me that.

VICKEY: I'm guessin' you're feelin' pretty conflicted right about now, ain't ya? At least I hope you are. I do have hope for you, Miss Jankowski. I am a Christian.

MAUREEN: Put that out.

(VICKEY *extinguishes her cigarette after taking a ceremonious last puff.*)

VICKEY: Why don't you make yourself about as scarce as you were when we all went to Richmond?

MAUREEN: I tried to be there.

VICKEY: Johnny was lookin' for you all over. It's a good thing he didn't find you after all they did to us without tellin' nobody.

MAUREEN: So he's upset?

VICKEY: Hates your guts.

(*There is the sound of pots crashing in the kitchen.* PHIL *enters covered with flour.*)

PHIL: I'm cooking. Margie's hungry.

(JONATHAN *enters.* PHIL *exits back into the kitchen.* VICKEY *hurries to* MAUREEN, *opposite side to where* JONATHAN *stands.*)

VICKEY: (*Harsh whisper*) He doesn't know.

MAUREEN: What?

VICKEY: (*Whispering*) He don't know.

JONATHAN: I don't know what?

VICKEY: That it was me smokin' that cigarette you're smellin'. It was horrible. Tasted like foul hogtail. I'll never touch another cigarette for as long as I live, I swear. That's what you didn't know— (*Glaring at* MAUREEN) And that's *all* you need to not know.

JONATHAN: So long as you'll never touch another one—

VICKEY: I won't. But the only reason I ever even smoked a cigarette was 'cause I saw her doin' it. That's why she's just leavin, right?

JONATHAN: Vickey, what's gotten into you?

VICKEY: *Who's* more like it.

JONATHAN: (*To* MAUREEN) I saw Jeb Sayer in town wearin' a new prosthetic leg you must've given him. His answer to how he came round to wearin' it surprised me. See, it seems he'd been punishin' himself for outlivin' his wife, feelin' bad 'cause his way of livin' should've made him the one to check out first. He says you shown a light on his selfishness and he wasn't even thinkin' about the wishes of the one he was purporting to love so much. He said his wife came to him in a dream and called him on his selfishness and that he owed her him living a life without her. From that point he's been wearin' it, on account of selfishness.

MAUREEN: Often self-righteousness should be called selfish-righteousness.

JONATHAN: Well, he's certainly feelin' good about all you've done for him.

MAUREEN: As will you.

JONATHAN: I've crossed that bridge already.

VICKEY: (*Pointedly loud*) Maureen, you know what those doctors told us when we left that hospital? That we all had a clean bill of health. That was the full extent of everything they said and that's all Johnny needed to know. That's all he knows 'cause that's all he heard. I made sure of it, do you understand me?

MAUREEN: (*Finally getting it*) I think I do.

VICKEY: And now you oughta git.

JONATHAN: Vickey, what the hell is wrong with you? And don't tell me I don't want to know—I want to know.

VICKEY: No, you don't.

JONATHAN: I—

MAUREEN: They performed more than physicals.

JONATHAN: What?

VICKEY: *(To* MAUREEN*)* Damn—you!

JONATHAN: I'll say it again—what?

MAUREEN: You need to know this in the event there are complications.

VICKEY: You ain't seen complications yet.

JONATHAN: Tell me. Physicals. Psych. IQ tests. What else is there?

MAUREEN: Birth control.

JONATHAN: We've been over this already.

MAUREEN: There was an extra procedure.

*(*JONATHAN *stands puzzled.)*

VICKEY: Bogota, Johnny, Bogota. Good ol' Bogota, US of A.

JONATHAN: *(To* MAUREEN*)* You *fixed* them?

MAUREEN: It was the only way I could let you keep them.

JONATHAN: And that's legal?

MAUREEN: In 1975 it's the law. You would have fought it, John. Then Margie, Phil, Kyle—they would have taken them away from you and you were never going to get them back. That's what you told me was most important to you and I fought for that with everything I had. And I got you that.

JONATHAN: They were barely there for a day.

MAUREEN: Dr Fleming should have done this years ago.

JONATHAN: But then he couldn't—

VICKEY: That's why we met you outside the hospital, Johnny. I didn't want you knowin' what they did.

JONATHAN: And why not me? I'm their son, I've got their genes?

MAUREEN: The State doesn't see you as mentally ill.

JONATHAN: Neither are they.

MAUREEN: It's what the State sees.

MARGIE: *(To* MAUREEN*)* What did you do to me?

MAUREEN: Something good, Margie. You'll thank me.

JONATHAN: You didn't give her a choice! YOU DIDN'T GIVE ANY OF THEM A CHOICE!!

(KYLE *enters.)*

KYLE: Reen! Reen!

MAUREEN: No, Kyle, not now—

KYLE: Reen!

MAUREEN: I said no, Kyle—leave me alone—

KYLE: Come, come swing.

MAUREEN: Not now, understand me, Kyle, not now.

JONATHAN: She's no better than Dr Fleming, Kyle. All she sees is a little white mouse to experiment on. You don't exist, you're not a real person. Same for you, Margie. And you, Phil, you're a nude mouse.

PHIL: I'm a man, Johnny.

JONATHAN: What about Vickey?

MAUREEN: I've done good here, John.

JONATHAN: What about my little sister? You fixed her? You neutered her?

MAUREEN: She's a ward of the State.

JONATHAN: You fixed her?

MAUREEN: Yes.

(Beat)

JONATHAN: I feel like such an idiot. I was under the stupid assumption that you came back here because you cared about me, and that maybe you had figured out a way for me to have everything, Maureen.

MAUREEN: I would like to try. It's complicated, but there's a way. I really do like you, Jonathan, and I want to get to know you, and help you and I think you can help me. I know what I've done may sound horrible to you, but in time you'll see it was for the best and you'll stop hating me and maybe you might even appreciate me. And maybe you'll let me be a part of what you have here. There's so much good I can do here, if you'll let me.

JONATHAN: I just want to ask one thing of you—warn us before you do any more good. Now, get— *(He begins to shake, as the seconds tick by the shaking increases in intensity.)*

VICKEY: Johnny? Johnny?

*(*JONATHAN *falls to the floor, convulsing.)*

MAUREEN: What is it?

VICKEY: Complications!

(As VICKEY *struggles to hold* JONATHAN *still, she's joined by* PHIL, *who gives* VICKEY *a bite stick that she places in* JONATHAN's *mouth.)*

PHIL: Son?

(Lights to black)

(End of Scene 5)

Scene 6

(The next morning early. MAUREEN *sits upright in a chair asleep.)*

*(*KYLE *carries a large box down the stairs.* VICKEY *follows with another box. They exit through the front door, past the sleeping* MAUREEN. *She wakens as* KYLE *and* VICKEY *re-enter.)*

VICKEY: *(Continuing; to* KYLE*)* You don't rest till we get the truck loaded.

*(*KYLE *exits up the stairs.)*

VICKEY: There's hot coffee in the kitchen.

MAUREEN: Coffee doesn't increase John's seizures?

VICKEY: No, just you.

MAUREEN: Does he have them often?

VICKEY: Would you believe me if I told you hardly never? *(Then)* I suppose we're done for now, ain't we? You're probably thinkin' right now that a man with epilepsy ain't fit for the task at hand.

MAUREEN: You're right, I'm thinking.

VICKEY: John always warned me not to joke about serious things and I guess having a baby is serious. I was only tryin' to have some fun with you, but all I did was spook you into doing what you did.

MAUREEN: I wasn't spooked.

VICKEY: An' I ain't never really thought about having babies—but all night it's all that was in my head. Will I ever stop thinking about it?

MAUREEN: You'll be too busy living your life, Vickey, having fun.

(JONATHAN *enters from upstairs, scattered and still a little dazed.*)

VICKEY: Speakin' of fun, look what the cat drug in. (*After a beat, she exits up the stairs.*)

MAUREEN: You had a seizure while you were at the U, didn't you?

JONATHAN: A bad one.

MAUREEN: You were embarrassed.

JONATHAN: Humiliated.

MAUREEN: So you threw in the towel.

JONATHAN: After the freak show I put on, towels were everywhere.

MAUREEN: Not very tough.

JONATHAN: Never said I was.

MAUREEN: Are your seizures followed by migraines?

JONATHAN: Just call it a headache.

(*Beat*)

MAUREEN: You skipped your meds.

JONATHAN: Jeez, now you're thinkin' I can't—that this—it won't happen again, okay? After you're gone I'll have nothing to distract me.

MAUREEN: What would happen if Phil and Margie one day they forgot about contraception? Would Margie have an abortion or carry it to term? Why risk putting her through that—assuming Roe v. Wade is never overturned. And if she carried it to term, what happens to you, John? I think you'll find no amount of love is going to remedy the life you never had. And Vickey will grow up now and get married, and if she feels she must have children then she can adopt a healthy child. And Kyle—why take the risk?

JONATHAN: Why? You're looking at it. You never know for sure just what miracle could occur, but the problem is you don't believe in miracles.

(MARGIE *enters ahead of* PHIL. *They are in costume and laden with large boxes.*)

MARGIE: Good morning.

PHIL: Good morning.

MARGIE: Let's hurry, Phillip.

JONATHAN: Margie, Phil, wait.

MARGIE: We'll be late.

JONATHAN: We're not going to the fair.

PHIL: I'm goin'.

JONATHAN: Phil, what's the point?

PHIL: I worked for it, I'm goin'.

JONATHAN: They don't care about us, Phil.

PHIL: You don't wanna go, okay. Today we go to the Fair. I'll drive.

MARGIE: You'll kill us.

PHIL: We'll get there.

JONATHAN: It's off, everything is off—your whole lives are off, the fair is off!

PHIL: Because you say so?

JONATHAN: It won't be real business.

PHIL: That ain't it! I wanna. I got a—I got a—

MARGIE: Right.

JONATHAN: You don't have any rights! You're lab rats!

MARGIE: You can kiss my ass, Jonathan Gallagher.

MAUREEN: Seizure—withdrawal—self-pity? That the pattern?

JONATHAN: Dominate. Manipulate. Castrate. That your pattern?

(VICKEY *and* KYLE *enter dressed in their costumes.* VICKEY *carries* JONATHAN's *costume, handing it him.*)

VICKEY: You are crazy if you think we're not going to that Renaissance Fair, Jonathan Gallagher. Put that costume on.

(*Off* JONATHAN's *hesitation:*)

VICKEY: Did you hear what I said?

(*As* JONATHAN *slowly puts the costume over his clothes,* PHIL *sets the box down, removes a vase and hands it to her.*)

MAUREEN: How much?

PHIL: It's a gift.

MAUREEN: It's signed "Norman Rockwell".

PHIL: We like Norman Rockwell.

(*Pause. They all look to* JONATHAN.)

JONATHAN: Let's go to the fair.

PHIL: I was goin' anyway.

(JONATHAN *digs in the credenza for an instamatic camera. He hands this to* MAUREEN.)

JONATHAN: Would you take a photograph of us? I've had something planned for a long time.

(*He puts a pair of sunglasses on everyone and gathers them together in a pose.*)

JONATHAN: A portrait of the Blues Family.

MAUREEN: Do you want to smile, Phil?

PHIL: I'm too cool to smile, Maureen.

(MAUREEN *snaps a photograph.*)

MAUREEN: And one more for me. (*She snaps another.*)

JONATHAN: All right, everybody, we have to hurry if we're to get there in time. Let's go.

(VICKEY, MARGIE, PHIL *and* KYLE *exit.*)

(JONATHAN *sets a large stack of papers and envelopes on the table in front of* MAUREEN.)

MAUREEN: What are these?

JONATHAN: Those are Dr Fleming's files, every note, every thought, every thing he ever did from the time Margie and Phil were younger than Vickey till the day he died.

MAUREEN: Are Margie and Phil—

JONATHAN: Just read. And when you're through reading, lock the door behind you. If we could survive him, we can survive you.

MAUREEN: John—what happened to Dr Fleming? How did he die?

JONATHAN: Cardiac arrhythmia—a retarded heartbeat.

(JONATHAN *exits.* MAUREEN *turns a page in a journal. As a flurry of emotions ignites in her—*)

(*Lights to black*)

(*Curtain*)

END OF PLAY